THE TEN COMMANDMENTS

The Ten Commandments

Covenant of Love

ALFRED McBRIDE, O. PRAEM.

ST. ANTHONY MESSENGER PRESS

Cincinnati, Ohio

Nihil Obstat: Donald Miller, O.F.M.

Imprimi Potest: Fred Link, O.F.M.
  Provincial

Imprimatur: +Most Rev. Carl K. Moeddel, V.G.
  Archdiocese of Cincinnati
  January 25, 2001

The *nihil obstat* and *imprimatur* are a declaration that a book is considered to be free from doctrinal or moral error. It is not implied that those who have granted the *nihil obstat* and *imprimatur* agree with the contents, opinions or statements expressed.

publishers and the Trustees of Amherst College; "Are We Happy
Yet?" by Stan Grossfeld, *The Boston Globe Magazine,* January 18,
1997, reprinted courtesy of *The Boston Globe;* "Living Chastely in
College" by Kimberly R. Bucher, reprinted with permission of
Crisis magazine; "A Prophet's Vision and Grace" by Vicky
Kemper, with Larry Engle, *Sojourners,* December 1987, reprinted
with permission from *Sojourners.*

Cover design by Mary Alfieri
Cover photo art by P. Price, copyright ©Digital Vision
Book design by Sandy L. Digman
Pagination and electronic format by Sandy L. Digman

ISBN 0-86716-376-3

Contents

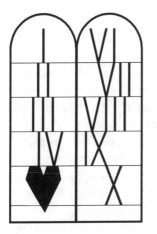

Introduction

To keep the Ten Commandments is to be faithful to God. But it is also to be faithful to ourselves, to our authentic nature and our deepest aspirations. Before being written in stone, these commandments were inscribed in the heart of man as the universal moral law. God's laws are not arbitrary commands, but guidelines set forth by a loving Father who cares for the welfare of his child and understands the most urgent promptings of his heart.

— POPE JOHN PAUL II, DURING HIS PILGRIMAGE TO MOUNT SINAI, MARCH 2000

How shall I live? This question arises again and again in all our lives. How shall I relate to God and people? Answers to the question come at us from a variety of sources. Therapists, philosophers, TV talk-show guests, writers of advice columns in newspapers tell us what they think we should do.

The shelves of bookstores bulge with hundreds of self-help books. People hunger to know about themselves and how to be happy. The majority of these books provide immediate and partial guides on how to be moral and happy. Most, but not all, of the responses today propose solutions that have little to do with God or the ultimate

1

meaning of life. It is rare, in a secular age, to find public replies that draw from the wisdom of the Ten Commandments.

There is no way to escape rules. Just look at H. Jackson Brown, Jr.'s *Life's Little Instruction Book* (Nashville, Tenn.: Rutledge Hill Press, 2000), a collection of fatherly advice for his son. "Praise in public. Criticize in private. Don't rain on other people's parades. Put the cap back on the toothpaste. Refill the ice cube trays. Do nice things for people who will never find out it was you." Rules like these appeal to people because they teach consideration for others. Far from being burdens, they lighten the load of daily life.

When a rich young man came to Jesus to ask about the right way to live, he heard Jesus say, "If you would enter into life, keep the commandments" (Matthew 19:17). Jesus proceeded to put the commandments in context. He spoke of goodness that can be achieved by communion with God, who is the source of goodness. Our society seems to hold that we can be morally good without God. Jesus would say we need to be in touch with the source of goodness—God —so we can be good.

He also invited the young man to discipleship. He should sell all and follow Jesus. This would involve a personal surrender in order to be transformed spiritually. This is what is meant by sacrificial love. In Scripture the sacrificial lamb was surrendered to the fire and transformed into an offering pleasing to God. Jesus surrendered himself to the Father by mounting the fire of the cross to be transformed into the risen Lord. Our discipleship is just such a surrender and is an intimate part of living the moral life.

Communion with God and becoming a disciple of Christ constitute the environment in which we approach the commandments. Rules alone are not enough. They should flow from a communion with God and a decision to be a follower of Jesus. There is a loving framework with the Father and the Son within which we see how the commandments work. There is also the power of the Holy Spirit given to us so that we are affectionately sealed with love that makes keeping the commandments a light yoke and a sweet burden.

First Comes Covenant

Scripture speaks of this framework as covenant. At Sinai God first proposed a covenant of love before giving the commandments. God reminds Moses about all the acts of love that God had performed for Israel—the liberation from Egypt, manna in the wilderness, water from a rock and quail from the skies and so on. "You have seen for yourselves how I treated the Egyptians and how I bore you up on eagle wings and brought you here to myself" (Exodus 19:4).

Having reviewed his gifts of love for them, God asks the Israelites to enter into a communion of goodness—a covenant—which would result in their becoming his beloved people. "If you hearken to my voice and keep my covenant, you shall be my special possession, dearer to me than all other people" (Exodus 19:5).

In the name of his people, Moses agreed and concluded a covenant with God. Only then did God give Moses the Ten Commandments. They were meant to be ways to live out the covenant. These commands were God's answer to the question, "How shall I live?" But they are never meant to be understood apart from communion with God, discipleship of Christ and covenant.

Hence it is clear that biblical morality does not begin with the commandments. It starts with the covenant at Sinai, after which the commandments are given. God gives Israel his love and invites a surrender of love in return. Jesus repeated this process and completed his covenant of love in a new and perfect manner on Calvary's hill and in the garden of the Resurrection.

In his Sermon on the Mount (Matthew 5—7) Jesus gives us a new and striking interpretation of the Ten Command-

3

ments. Beginning with eight roads to real happiness through the practice of the Beatitudes, Jesus breaks open the commandments and reveals their inner beauty and the way they apply to our inner attitudes as well as our external behavior.

Through his death and resurrection, Jesus perfected the divine covenant that began at Sinai. The difference between Sinai and Calvary is that now we have the Holy Spirit to seal our covenant with God and enable us to be moral. Through the Spirit's presence in us, the risen Jesus becomes our moral teacher.

In its presentation of the Ten Commandments, the *Catechism of the Catholic Church* (CCC) is equally clear. The *Catechism* begins its coverage of morality by dealing with the two commandments of Christ about the love of God and loving our neighbor as we love ourselves.

Christ's commandments are covenant statements. The *Catechism* places the first three commandments under Christ's call to love God with all our mind, heart and strength. It introduces the last seven commandments with Christ's call to love our neighbor.

Commandments Humanize Us

We will also find the commandments more helpful when we realize they are designed to meet our human need for true fulfillment. God is the author of human nature, and knows what will contribute to its positive and creative development. Every commandment contains a value that makes us better human beings.

Honoring parents leads to treasuring family values. Reverence for human life opens us to spreading peace in the world. Marital commitment reveals the jewel of fidelity that nourishes spousal love. Respect for property discloses the deeper virtue of social justice that gives all people the means to protect their human dignity. Telling the truth engenders trust, without which no society can survive.

The commandments have a positive and a negative side. The acts that are forbidden draw attention to what will dehumanize us. But each commandment has a positive side, virtues of faith, reverence, family, life, love, justice, truth, chastity and generosity that make us noble in the practice. Obeying the commandments humanizes us and opens our hearts to God and our final destiny.

When we have answered the call to communion, discipleship and covenant, we will find the commandments the next logical step. After all, it is one thing to tell someone, "I love you." Then it is necessary to show the beloved that you mean it. Loving acts must follow loving words.

In this short course on the Ten Commandments I have introduced each commandment with a story designed to evoke the feeling the commandment contains. Then I pose a question about keeping the commandment. This is followed by three strategies taken from the *Catechism*. Each strategy is developed separately and followed by some form of reflection exercise.

Everything is arranged in such a way that this course can be self-taught individually or used in a group setting. The think pieces and the exercises that accompany them keep the action focused on personal and communal faith, life and practice. There are a number of passages from the *Catechism*, which throw light on the given topics and allow their meanings to unfold for you. I hope you will be intrigued enough to read and pray over the full selections cited from the *Catechism*.

Follow Jesus

Keeping the commandments is important so long as we understand that following Jesus is the point of it all. This is the real key to the moral life. This is why we agree to a Gospel teaching or observe a biblical commandment. When we surrender to the person of Jesus, we share in his free and loving obedience to the Father's will.

Jesus asks us to follow him and imitate his path of love, in which we give of ourselves to others out of enthusiastic love for God. Following Jesus goes beyond the external imitation of Christ's behavior. It refers to an interior transformation into Jesus himself. Following him includes three calls: Lose the self. Take the cross. Follow Christ.

Taking the cross implies that we open ourselves to letting Jesus live his humility, obedience, and saving death and resurrection within us. When these acts begin to shape our inner lives, then the following of Jesus shows us what the moral life is all about. An immoral world has no time for the cross. In fact, it invented the cross to punish those who would stand for morality and perfect love for God and neighbor.

Following Jesus is no amiable, user-friendly morality. It is as tough as the nails that impaled Jesus on the wood. But from that came the glorious joy of the Resurrection. It is the true and final answer to our perennial question.

How shall I live?

That's the question.

Jesus has given us the answer.

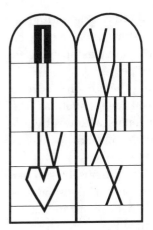

First Commandment

Love God

'I, the LORD am your God....You shall not have other gods besides me.... 'you shall love the LORD, your God, with all your heart, and with all your soul, and with all your strength.' —DEUTERONOMY 5:6-7; 6:5

'I Will Return to Earth to Teach People to Love Love'

What do you say about a twenty-four-year-old nun who died of tuberculosis? In the case of Saint Thérèse of Lisieux, plenty. But that was not the opinion of the Carmelite sisters outside her sickroom. "Thérèse will die soon. What will the prioress put in her obituary? 'She entered our convent, lived and died.' There really isn't much else to say."

Yet within a few months of her death, such a storm of interest and affection for Thérèse began that a Vatican cardinal declared, "We must hasten to canonize Thérèse, otherwise the people will go ahead and do it without us."

What accounted for the enormous interest in her? It was the publication of her spiritual journal, *The Story of a Soul*. It became an immediate, worldwide best-seller and revealed her story.

Her advice was simplicity itself: What is important is

not great deeds but rather to do everyday acts with great love for God and neighbor. "I will return to earth to teach people to love Love." Her love of God was absolute. It found practical expression in love of people.

Millions have felt the love that Thérèse promised to teach and returned it with enthusiasm, such as the Madagascar orphans and Japanese lepers who went without rice to make a donation to build a basilica for her in Lisieux.

African priests in the Congo placed themselves under her protection, and a Canadian city sent a thousand pilgrims to celebrate the anniversary of her canonization.

And in Iran, a Shiite Moslem, whose faith forbids images of God or prophets, kept a picture publicly posted of the Thérèse who brought him a cure. Said he, "Neither Mohammed nor the prophets outweigh this lovely saint."

Pope John Paul II has named her a doctor of the Church, the third woman to be so named. To celebrate this occasion, a portion of her relics toured the world. In this symbolic manner the cloistered woman is still teaching us to do the ordinary thing with extraordinary love.

Thérèse's story is a living illustration of the First Commandment.

Do You Love God?

The *Catechism* (CCC) offers us three ways to say yes to this question:

- Jesus made the love of God his first commandment (page 9).

- Our love for God should be wholehearted (page 16).

- We should not love false gods (page 21).

• JESUS MADE THE LOVE OF GOD HIS FIRST COMMANDMENT. (*CCC*, 2084-2094)

The story of Saint Thérèse highlights the way in which she lived the love of God. Her life illumined the ultimate meaning of the First Commandment, as it is found both in the rules given to Moses and in the teaching of Jesus.

Love of God and people sums up the moral life. The Ten Commandments (also called the Decalogue) reflect this teaching. The *Catechism* explains it this way:

> When someone asks him, "Which commandment in the Law is the greatest?" Jesus replies: "You shall love the Lord your God with all your heart, and with all your soul and with all your mind. This is the greatest and first commandment. And a second is like it: You shall love your neighbor as yourself..." The Decalogue must be interpreted in the light of this twofold yet single commandment of love.... (*CCC*, 2055)

The first three commandments are about the love of God. The last seven deal with the love of people.

Here we reflect upon the first commandment of the Decalogue, which is mirrored by Jesus in his first commandment to love God above all else. Spousal love is one of the ways in which we can appreciate the way we can come to love God. The following story gives us a hint.

Shall We Dance?

Boris Castell was a hero. He lived to be eighty-seven. Why do we call him a hero? What made him a hero?

We normally associate heroism with courage, whether that is shown in competitive athletics or on the battlefield of war. Boris was born into a European aristocratic family with all the privileges that came with it. He attended the best schools, learned seven languages and earned a doctorate in chemistry.

He was an academic hero.

He competed in the 1936 Olympics in Berlin where he saw Hitler leave the stadium after the African-American Jesse Owens won the gold medal. Boris went up to Jesse and congratulated him for his victory. Boris also competed in the winter Olympics that year in cross-country skiing.

He was an athletic hero.

In World War II, he joined the underground and fought against the Nazis. He was tireless and brave as he risked his life to turn back the tide of evil unleashed by Hitler. Boris was an atheist who one day found himself hiding out in a Catholic monastery. Huddled in a monk's robe, he sat in the Church, which had no other light but a paschal candle. He found himself strangely moved by the light and began to question himself. Is Jesus really what his followers say he is? Is he a savior? Is he worthy of love? The answer would come later.

He was a war hero.

After the war, Boris felt such a bitter hatred for the Nazis that he joined a secret group of Nazi hunters who roamed South America looking for them and turning them in to the authorities. One day he met a Jewish family who gave him a package to bring back to New York and give to their daughter. Her name was Eva, and she ran a dance studio.

Boris brought the gift to the studio. When he saw Eva, a "Jewish Princess," he fell in love with her—and she with him. They began seeing each other during the few months he had in the city before returning to South America. Friends urged him to allow Eva to teach him to dance in her studio so that they could dance together. But he somehow understood that were he to do this he would lose the hatred he held tightly in his heart. He did not want to let it go.

The day came for him to leave. He was at the airport, tormented at losing Eva yet committed to what he deemed was a just cause. As he debated with himself, he recalled the lighted candle from the monastery. He uttered his first

10

prayer, "Jesus take away the hatred in my heart. Fill it with love." Repeating the prayer over and over, he felt the hatred draining from his being. He left the airport, took a taxi back to the studio and went in. Eva was there. He went up to her and bowed in his courtly, European manner and said, "Shall we dance?"

They married and grew in love year by year. Soon thereafter, Boris and Eva entered the Rite of Christian Initiation for Adults (RCIA) and became Catholics. They spent the remainder of their active days teaching religion and English in a Catholic high school. This miracle of love between a man and woman is an image of the mystery of love for God to which we are all called.

Boris became a hero of love for God—as did Eva.

When playwright David Hare interviewed clergy as part of his research for his play *Racing Demons,* he faced a problem. None of the clerics wanted to talk about loving God. They only felt easy when discussing the love of people.

Jesuit Father Edward Collins Vacek encountered the same difficulty when he asked his students what they meant by love of God. "They usually gave one of four answers. Some volunteered that loving God means keeping the commandments, like not killing or stealing. Most say that loving God means helping one's neighbor. The more theologically educated add that it means taking care of the poor. Lastly, those steeped in our psychological age share that loving God means caring for one's deepest self. All seem not to notice that atheists affirm these four practices" ("The Eclipse of Love for God," *America* [3 March 1996]).

Without a doubt, we are commanded to love people. But just as certainly, the first commandments of Moses and Jesus say we should love God directly—and not only indirectly through people. In his Last Judgment sermon (Matthew 25:31-46), Jesus says the Christian standard of judgment is richer than humanistic, ethical demands. Yes, it is important to feed the hungry, clothe the naked and give water to the thirsty. But this should be done as if given to Christ himself.

Romano Guardini clarifies this when he writes, "Not love, then, is the measure, but *that love which is directed to Jesus Christ*....In daily life we deal with people as they come to us. But behind each of them, says Jesus, stands God. Christ came to make each life his own, and now all that happens to that life runs through him" (*The Lord* [Washington, D.C.: Regnery Publishing, Inc., 1996], 340). Our neighbor loving, commendable as it is, should open us to a personal and loving relationship with God.

How can we learn to love God directly?

The *Catechism* teaches that the virtues of faith and hope lead us to the virtue of love for God.

Faith

I will love God when I experience his love for me. God has planted signs of his love in creation. "The heavens declare the glory of God" (Psalms 19:1). The beauty of the stars at night and the sun at dawn appeal to our desire for loveliness. The visible beauty of creation leads us to the Creator. A lover likes to send roses to the beloved. God is a lover who adorns our earthly home with mountains and oceans and gardens. Each sign is a card that says, "I love you."

And when we look within ourselves, we discover a conscience that wants to judge what is right and wrong. We notice the drive of our minds that never stop searching for truth. We feel the surge of our hearts that teem with desire for nothing less than the infinite. Our inner life is a love gift from God. We are dynamic because God made us that way. The seed of love in our hearts will never stop unfolding until we reach God. Only sin can stop us from doing this.

Finally, God knew that creation and the powers of the soul would not be enough. A lover wants to reveal himself. Being the greatest lover of all, God chose to reveal himself, first to the patriarchs and the prophets, then in Jesus Christ his only Son, to the apostles and disciples. Scripture calls Jesus God's Word. In that Word, God says, "I love you so much that I show you who I am in my Son, Jesus."

Our response to God's love is in the act of faith. Powerful though he is, God can only offer us his love. We must be willing to accept it. That is what faith does. Our faith is a personal yes to the divine affection for us. In this act, we are not yet returning our love to God. We are content to let his love change us, warm our souls and make us into his beloved. It is like allowing the light of the sun to nourish us. The first step in our love relationship to God is permitting the Lord to love us. This is the wondrous work of faith. It is a time for enjoying being loved.

Hope

When God shows us his love, we soon realize that we can scarcely return a love that would match the divine energy that has opened up to us. How shall we be able to give love back to God? We must hope that God will also give us the capacity to love him in return. "Hope is the confident expectation of divine blessing..." (CCC, 2090).

Hope moves us to beg for the ability to love him back. Saint Thomas Aquinas says that our love is an affection for the good that we notice. This is true whether we possess the good or we do not. When we have the good, as in the case of God's love, we delight in it. When we do not have the good, we hope for it. Love is our elemental driving force pushing us toward God. This is all the more true the day we wake up and feel God's love eagerly at our door wanting to give us everything we need to be truly fulfilled.

The divine lover will never leave us at rest. Once we are touched by the fire, we feel ourselves motivated to dig deeply into the goodness of God. Our lover is not forcing us to come to him. He places before us the enchantment of his goodness exactly suited to the desire planted within us. When our inborn yearning meets its proper goal, it rises up and goes for the gold. God has touched us with his magic, and we spontaneously turn toward that love that we have hoped for. We also hoped to have the capacity to love, and God has generously provided us with precisely that gift.

Charity

Here we arrive at the very essence of the First Commandment. The highest form of the love we may have for God is *agape* love.

This is a selfless love in which we love God for his sake alone. Jesus presented this love in terms of discipleship and the cross. So great should be our love for God that we would be willing to die for him if necessary. The sign of the cross expresses our highest love for God.

At the same time, there is another kind of love we could have for God, and that is *eros* love. This refers to loving God for our own sake. The traditional act of contrition explains the difference between agape and eros. We are heartily sorry because our sins have offended God. This is agape. But we could mainly be sorry because we would experience loss of heaven and the pains of hell. This is eros. It is not as great as agape, but it still is truly love for God, genuinely biblical and Catholic. We love God for the good that we acquire in being close to God.

Finally, there is *philia* love. This is friendship love. We love God for the sake of the friendship we want to have with God. Here we deal with our relationship with God. Scripture is clear about the Jews having a covenant bond with God, a relationship that makes them friends of God. The Bible also notes that in Baptism we experience a covenant relationship with Christ. We want to be his friends. To make this possible, we say our prayers, sing in church, work in a soup kitchen, try to be kind to people. Unbelievers may do many of these things—other than churchgoing. The difference is that we do it to maintain a friendship with God.

Our first answer to the question, "Do you love God?" is based upon the way in which we respond to the first com-

14

mandment of both Moses and Jesus, namely, to love God. We have seen that many people find it more practical to love people and seem ill at ease with loving God directly. Since love of people is also a commandment, that seems like a satisfactory substitute.

But as we reflect on the commandment, we become more aware that a love relationship with God is both necessary and totally fulfilling. The virtues of faith and hope lead us to the virtue of love in its threefold form of agape, eros and philia.

So we begin our meditation on the First Commandment with a call to accept and experience God's love and then beg the graces we need to return that love in ever more intense self-giving.

Life Application

1) Read again the opening story about Saint Thérèse. She is the saint of love for God and others. When you hear her words, "I will return to earth to teach people to love Love," what reaction do you have to her words? How might they awaken in you a renewed desire to love God? Why can we say that the spousal love in the Boris and Eva story is an image of God's love for us?

2) What does it mean to you to have love for God? When have you had difficulty loving God directly? When have you had a tendency to pay more attention to neighbor loving than God loving?

3) God plants signs of his love for us in the beauty of creation and in the activity of our minds, hearts and consciences. God has gone further and directly revealed his love through the prophets and apostles and in the person of his son, Jesus Christ. How have you been affected by God's love manifested in creation? How have you noticed God's love in the activities of your soul? How has God's formal revelation as found in

Scripture shown you his love for you? How have you responded to these various advances from God?

• OUR LOVE FOR GOD SHOULD BE WHOLEHEARTED. (CCC, 2095-2109)

God Wants All Your Rooms

The Father knocks at my door seeking a home for his son.
Rent is cheap, I say.
I don't want to rent. I want to buy, says God.
I'm not sure I want to sell, but you might come in to look.
I think I will, says God.
I might let you have a room or two.
I like it, says God, I'll take the two.
I'd like to give you more. I need some space for me.
I know, says God, but I'll wait. I like what I see.
Hmm. Maybe I can let you have another room.
  I really don't need that much.
Thanks, says God. I'll take it.
I'd like to give you the whole house, but I'm not sure.
Think on it, says God. I wouldn't put you out.
  Your house would be mine and my son would live in it.
  You'd have more space than you had before.
I don't understand at all.
I know, says God, but I can't tell you about that.
  You'll have to discover it for yourself.
That can only happen if you let him have the whole house.
A bit risky, I say.
Yes, says God, but try me.
I'm not sure.
I'll let you know.
I can wait, says God. I like what I see.
—FROM "COVENANT," BY MARGARET HALASKA, O.S.F.

Moses teaches that we shall serve only the true God. Jesus quotes Deuteronomy 6:4 to point out that we ought to love God with all our heart. In the little dialogue cited above, we see that God wants all the rooms in the house of our soul. God proposes this plan. He does not impose it. In the First Commandment, God plays for the highest stakes. God says to us, "My son, my daughter, give me your whole heart."

At the same time, God has exquisite timing. He never rushes the process of love. "I can wait." Love's advance is gentle, always waiting for the next moment of surrender. Our adventure is spelled out in weeks and years. For God, this is a blink of the eye. A thousand years are but a day with God.

How can we love God wholeheartedly?

By admitting our sinfulness.

By trusting that God alone can save us through his Son.

It is difficult to experience God's love if we fail to have an honest appreciation of our sinfulness. Jesus does not begin to speak to us about love but about conversion. "Repent, for the kingdom of heaven is at hand" (Matthew 4:17). Conversion from what? From actual sin.

Moral conversion requires we take a deep look at ourselves. What do we find? First, we would conclude there is something terribly wrong with us. Extreme examples of human sinfulness abound: the Holocaust, Hiroshima, Rwanda, Kosovo. Every day the newspapers report murder, rape, greed, cheating and injustices done to the weak and the poor.

Something is wrong with humanity. The Church teaches that this is the result of original sin. Baptism liberates us from original sin, but Baptism does not take away the damage. It's a little like scar tissue. The operation succeeded, but a scar abides. The effects of original sin remain—darkened minds, weakened wills, riotous emotions, self-destructive attitudes. The originating evil still haunts us.

But this is not the whole story. There is also something grand and marvelous about us. "What is man that you should be mindful of him? ...You have made him little less than an angel, and crowned him with glory and honor" (Psalms 8:5a-6). Our humanity has produced a Mother

17

Teresa, John Paul II, Martin Luther King and Gandhi. We have become aware of our moral responsibility to society, to obtain justice that there might be peace, to honor the human dignity of every man and woman on earth.

The aftershocks of original sin are not the only inner pressure that affect us. There is a positive force inside us, pure and mighty, that surges from the truth that we are images of God. For "the fruit of the Spirit is love, joy, peace, patience, kindness, generosity, faithfulness, gentleness, [and] self-control" (Galatians 5:22). Our identity with God pushes us beyond lies to seek truth, urges us to believe in fidelity despite all betrayals, convinces us that love is possible regardless of the hatreds we have known.

Our lives then are marked by the twin poles of originating evil and the dynamic force of being God's images.

This is experienced as a moral conflict that needs to be resolved. In our can-do American culture we naturally think we can solve this on our own. We live by the myth that heroic moral effort will deliver us from the moral quandary that upsets us. We support this illusion by trying out techniques of mystical insight or voraciously devouring knowledge. We are told that knowledge is power, so why not get as much as we can? We are educated to think we can be masters of the universe, therefore, let's get on with the conquest of self.

Father Robert Barron prescribes exactly the right medicine at this point. *"Sin,"* he writes, *"is not simply a weakness that can be overcome but rather a condition from which we have to be saved.* Again, this insight should not depress us. *Au contraire*, it should allow us, at an elemental psychological and spiritual level, to relax, to surrender, to let go.

"What happens so often in the hearts of sinners is a kind of clenching or tightening of the spirit as the mind and will strive to break out of the prison of fear. All of this stretching and straining serves only to throw the ego back on itself in a misery of failure and self reproach" (*And Now I See*, [New York: Crossroad Publishing Company, 1998],

50-51 [emphasis added]).

If we wonder why we may find it difficult to offer God wholehearted love, the solution can be traced to the condition of our souls. They are conflicted by the aftermath of original sin and the counter-energy that happily spills into our awareness of being images of God. But then we aggressively seek to resolve the dilemma by our own efforts that are always doomed.

As Father Barron eloquently testifies, sin is not a condition from which we can extricate ourselves by personal efforts, no matter how noble and well meant. We need to be saved by the grace of Christ. This demands something we fear to do, namely, surrendering to a power other than our own. We need to trust in Christ. But fear holds us back. Jesus urges us to convert, to believe in him, to trust he can save us. Once we are liberated, we begin to love.

The Buddhists teach that we should invite our fears in for tea. Face your fear. Look squarely at your anxieties. They are basically illusions, ghosts that are only too happy to keep us in the dark and stop us from being free. Conversion means we dive deeper than our fears to get in touch with the divine image that assures that we can be free to love God. Jesus comes with the Good News that there is another way to live, free from fear and regenerated with the capacity to love. We are ready now for the creative, dynamic and salvational act of wholehearted love for God.

It is at this point we begin to appreciate the *Catechism's* linkage of love for God with acts of adoration, praise, prayer, sacrifice and vows of total dedication. These expansive acts of the virtue of religion must first be watered with the stories of conversion. Doctrine's lofty vision will mean more to us when infused with the vision of the human person struggling through the darkness of the conflict between originating evil and being images of God. Doctrine's austere words jump to life when associated with the human dramas of conversion that are accompanied with the sweat of fear and tenuous attempts to trust Christ.

19

When these storms are weathered, we will be able to kneel before Jesus, as did the Wise Men at the Epiphany. We have been released for adoration because we can say, "My Jesus, I trust in you." We will know how to gather our souls in prayer. We will joyfully embrace sacrificial love because we would not be satisfied with anything less. And some, as through all of history, will become vowed men and women hoping to become pure gifts to God.

This is the process that leads to wholehearted love.

Life Application

1) To whom or to what have you given your whole heart? How did it happen? What is there about love that demands total consecration?

2) Why did we argue that self-examination is necessary for coming to love God with all our hearts? How do you react to the contention that the aftershocks of original sin still affect our lives? How else would you account for the tendencies to evil everyone experiences? What is your response to the conviction that we are images of God, a truth that accounts for our inner drive to truth, goodness, beauty, love and God?

3) When have you known the inner moral conflicts that torment us by moving us to both goodness and evil? Tell stories of people you know or have read about who have undergone spiritual conversions to Christ. What is the common thread that unites their narratives? What are ways that people can overcome their fears and trust in Christ? How do you read the statement that sin is not a weakness we can overcome; it is a condition from which we need to be saved?

• WE SHOULD NOT LOVE FALSE GODS.
(CCC, 2110-2128)

> Human life finds its unity in the adoration of the one God. The commandment to worship the Lord alone integrates man and saves him from an endless disintegration. (CCC, 2114)

Your God and Mine

In the winter of 1977, Oxford University invited Cardinal Suenens to give the university retreat. It was the first time a Catholic had been asked to do this since the Reformation. They housed the cardinal at Christ Church College, a place begun by Cardinal Wolsey and completed by Henry VIII.

Every day Suenens worked enthusiastically with student groups. Each evening he spoke to standing-room-only crowds in the venerable Sheldonian theater, designed by Christopher Wren and paid for by Sheldon, then the archbishop of Canterbury.

Suenens spoke on the theme "Your God and Mine." He told his listeners how he had been touched by God, Father, Son and Spirit. At the conclusion of his final conference, the audience rose and gave him a heartwarming standing ovation. Then they broke out into a soaring rendition of the great hymn "Come, Thou Spirit Divine." University officials testified they had never seen such an outpouring of faith within the living memory of their days there.

When a person is intoxicated with God, he will share Good News. Suenens came to Oxford with the Good News of Jesus Christ and touched people with Christ's love and presence. He opened their hearts to the true God and led them to plead for the arrival of the Spirit, "Come, Thou Spirit Divine." When there is Good News in the heart, there will be Good News on the lips. Full of the experience of God's love, we can scarcely keep it to ourselves. We will strive to tell the world about the love of God.

False Gods

Having emphasized the call to accept God's love and to return that love, the Catechism then turns to the issue of being sure we are loving a real God.

In biblical times, Israel was challenged to discern the true God from false ones. When the First Commandment was heard from Sinai, virtually all people believed in a god. The problem was not belief in *a* god but in *what kind* of a god. Through Moses, God asked Israel to believe in a deity who loved the people personally—a divinity who was unique and spiritual.

The great political and economic powers of the time worshiped gods who were either personifications of the forces of nature (the moon, the sun) or emblems of fertility (the serpent, the bull). To its credit, Israel, despite its political and numerical insignificance compared to the empire of the Moon to the east (Assyria) and the empire of the Sun to the west (Egypt), held on to its remarkable faith in God with admirable fortitude.

Archaeological excavations in Palestine have yielded no representations of God or of any human figure who might have served as a deity substitute. Some Israelites did use small nude female fertility statuettes of Astarte for charms to induce pregnancy and good crops, but these were deviations borrowed from their Canaanite neighbors, not faith statements about their real God. Israel would have many faith difficulties in the ensuing centuries, but the people's core belief in a unique, spiritual and loving God endured amazingly well.

Israel did not totally escape trying to humanize God. Hundreds of passages in the Hebrew Scriptures portray God as able to speak, hear, smell and laugh. They speak of God as having eyes, ears, hands, feet and arms. God feels joy, anger, jealousy, disgust and regret at certain courses of action. Somehow this human face of God never completely distracted Israel from its belief in the Lord's sublime spiritual nature.

That does not mean, of course, that Israel never lapsed into idolatry like other nations or failed to grow in faith. Sadly, its history testifies that the Israelites did at times run after other gods or grow cold in their covenant commitment to the real God of love. Even at Sinai itself, the people faltered and fashioned a golden bull calf to worship. Happily, God found saints and prophets willing to be filled with divine spiritual fire, who inspired the people to reform their lives and set out again on the journey of faith.

Contemporary America is a nation that believes in God. Polls and surveys consistently report that over ninety percent of Americans believe in God. "A *U.S. News* poll suggests that at the end of the twentieth century, the wealthiest, most powerful and best-educated country on Earth is still one of the most religious. From the White House on down, Americans are a people who believe in a benevolent God who hears prayers and is able to intervene in human events. Inextricably woven into our civic consciousness is a proud heritage that tells us we are a 'nation under God '" (*U. S. News & World Report* [4 April 1994], 48-49).

But there is a dark underside to this rosy picture. Officially God is acknowledged and worshiped regularly in thousands of churches, synagogues, mosques and temples. On the other hand, would you agree that many Americans find a way to worship false gods along with the true one?

A clue may be found in Christ's interpretation of the First Commandment in his Sermon on the Mount. "No one can serve two masters. He will either hate the one and love the other, or be devoted to one and despise the other. You cannot serve God and mammon" (Matthew 6:24). Read also verses 25-34 in which Jesus identifies the anxiety that accompanies an attachment to material goods. His words could easily apply to our "Age of Anxiety."

What is *mammon*? It is the Hebrew word for material possessions. It is often simply translated as money. In Scripture, the only time Israel created an idol was during the giving of the Ten Commandments at Sinai. While Moses communed with God, the Israelites constructed a golden calf—a symbol of money and material possessions. They danced around the image of gold, sang songs to it and praised it. In a sense, they were worshiping money.

Turn now to present-day America—religious in one way, yet furiously dedicated to money and material possessions in the other. Can we really serve God and mammon and be at peace in our hearts? The scriptural word for "serve" in this context means "be a slave to." A slave is a creature of the master. A slave has no time for himself. He belongs to his owner. When money and material possessions become our god, then money owns us. It is not too much of a stretch to claim this is a modern form of idolatry.

None of this is meant to argue that the whole culture has become idolatrous in the sense meant here. But it is reasonable to raise the question that the worship of money is a nationwide temptation that invites all of us to serious self-examination. "Man commits idolatry whenever he honors and reveres a creature in place of God, whether these be gods or demons (for example, satanism), power, pleasure, race, ancestors, the state, money, etc." (CCC, 2113).

Preachers often connect idolizing money to power and sex. They speak of sex goddesses. The ability of money to buy power—or access to it—is well documented. The sermons may be overheated, but the reality cuts close to the bone. Idolatry is not just a weakness of times past. It can flourish today just as easily.

Atheism and Agnosticism

Atheists deny there is any god to worship. They come in differing forms. Some are practical materialists who devote their energies to what happens here and now. Others believe that humans are ends in themselves with supreme control of their own history. A third group focus their attention on economic and social liberation. They hold that "religion, of its very nature, thwarts such emancipation by raising man's hopes in a future life, thus both deceiving him and discouraging him from working for a better form of life on earth" (*Gaudium et Spes*, 20, 2).

In a way, this is another type of idolatry. People are gods. The creature is a self-creator. Communism made this idea an article of faith and attempted to force millions to live this way. In the West, secularity tends to produce the same belief, promoting it by persuasion, especially through the media.

Unfortunately, people of faith who are careless about their religious knowledge and practice, or who fail in their social and moral life, can conceal the reality of a loving and caring God and so create the environment for atheism. At the same time, atheists' moral responsibility for their position depends on their intentions and the circumstances that brought them to this state.

Agnostics either argue that God cannot be known or say they have no way of telling. Some of them seem to be searching for God; some say they want to believe in God so much that they behave as if they do while harboring doubt; others are simply indifferent. They may not want to develop their moral conscience. Most times they are practical atheists.

Our third consideration about going after false gods or lapsing into atheism and agnosticism illustrates the radical departure from the dream of the First Commandment that can happen. Instead of probing the drama of love that can exist between ourselves and God, these people move as far away from it as they can. In so doing, they lose what could perfect their humanity and satisfy the longings of the human heart. These worlds without God eventually dehumanize the participants, undermine human dignity and sabotage the loving plan of God to save everyone.

Life Application

1) When you hear the word idolatry, what associations and stories come to your mind? Why is it legitimate to argue that false gods exist today just as much as in biblical times? Besides the false gods mentioned above, what are some others you can mention?

2) Share stories about people you know or have read about who seem to have made money their god. How did this happen in their lives? Why is it illusory to think that idolizing wealth automatically makes people happy? Read Matthew 6:24-34 about material possessions and anxiety. Cite examples that support Christ's words about anxiety as noted in our contemporary society. What impact does serving "mammon" have on family life, culture and loving relationships?

3) Where have you encountered practical or even ideological atheists in your experiences? What was it like? What did you think about them? What would you say to someone who tells you she is an agnostic? Why can we say that going after false gods or becoming atheists and agnostics deprives humans of their real potential?

Meditation

Saint Bernard taught there are four stages in developing a love for God:

1) I love myself for my own sake. I am self-centered and have no interest in God.

2) I love God for my own sake. I become aware of God and of my dependence on him. But I only turn to God to fulfill my needs. In most cases, this comes about through a vivid awareness of Jesus.

3) I begin to love God for his sake. I experience an attraction to God in worship, meditation and prayer. God's love for me becomes apparent and heartwarming. A personal relationship with Jesus becomes a powerful incentive at this stage.

4) I love myself solely for the sake of God. Now I best appreciate my origin and destiny in God. I am humbled by the incredible gift of divine love and feel my whole life has importance because of God.

The reason I can embark on this love journey is because God is always calling me with love and because he has put within me the capacity to respond. "The first commandment enjoins us to love God above everything and all creatures for him and because of him" (*CCC*, 2093).

Prayer

> *Jesus, you have called me to accept the love you have for me and you have given me the gift of being able to love you in return. I praise you for this call and gift and ask that I may always grow in love for you as I journey in faith to your kingdom. Take my hand and walk with me that I may never stray and go after false gods or let doubts or temptations to unbelief affect my commitment to you. Never give up on me, Lord.* AMEN.

> God loves us as if there were only one of us to love. (Saint Augustine)

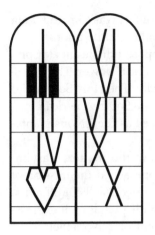

Second Commandment

Love God's Name

You shall not take the name of the LORD, your God, in vain.... Our Father in heaven,/hallowed be your name.

—DEUTERONOMY 5:11; MATTHEW 6:9

The Mission

When religion becomes so embroiled in politics that its spiritual nature and prophetic freedom to challenge the state and the culture are neutralized, then a wrong use of God's name is likely to occur. The film *The Mission* provides a heartbreaking example of such an outcome.

In 1750, Jesuit missionaries evangelized the Guarani Indians near the Iguazu Falls on what is now the border of Paraguay and Brazil. The missionaries created agricultural communes in which the Indians shared the fruits of their labors. They became commercial competitors with the neighboring Portuguese plantations that used Indian slave labor.

The Jesuits not only created a paradiselike "Mission Republic," they also discovered the Indians loved the classical music brought over from Europe. They formed Indian choirs and orchestras and trained them to make their own violins and other instruments. The effect was a breathtaking combination of agricultural and esthetic cultivation.

The royal courts of Europe opposed the Jesuits for presumed possession of too much political power. They pressured the pope to suppress the order. The Holy See judged that removing Jesuit control from the South American missions would pacify the kings as well as the jealous plantation owners.

A papal legate, sent to review the matter, was impressed by what he saw. As he approached the mission of San Carlos, the cardinal said, "A surgeon will cut off a diseased limb to save a life. I had no idea what an inexpressibly beautiful limb I was sent to cut off." Nonetheless, he ordered the mission closed, and the Jesuits returned to Europe.

He then had the dismaying experience of hearing about the colonists' massacre of the Indian population and the scorched-earth policy of the soldiers.

A landowner argued, "Your eminence, this is the way of the world."

"No," replied the cardinal, "We have made the world this way.... I have helped to make it so."

The story is a sad example of the *wrong use of God's name*. Religious authority was employed to close a mission that protected the Indians from slavery and introduced them to the dignity of communal farming and the beauty of art, architecture and music. The closing of the mission exposed the Indians to slaughter. The power of the sacred was subordinated to political ends.

'Do You Love God's Holy Name?'

The Catechism guides us to the truth of the matter in these ways.

- To reverence God's name is to respect the Person of God (page 31).

- There are numerous ways to make wrong use of God's name (page 35).

- Our Christian naming at Baptism calls us to holiness (page 40).

- **TO REVERENCE GOD'S NAME IS TO RESPECT THE PERSON OF GOD.** (*CCC*, 2142-2146)

The Power of One's Name

The story of *The Mission* is a good illustration of what the Second Commandment opposes. It dramatizes the wrong use of God's name. In the name of religion, a religious order, which was rescuing Indians from slavery and offering them a stable way of life in an environment of beauty and worship, was removed from the scene and the native population massacred.

Why is respecting a name so desirable?

Names have been important since the beginning of creation. After God created the animals, "he brought them to the man to see what he would call them; whatever the man called each of them would be its name" (Genesis 2:19).

Most people are more interested in their own names than anyone else's. They want others to pronounce their own names properly, and they dislike having their names misspelled. In certain fields, successful people attribute part of their accomplishments to their mastery of other people's names. There is an old saying about bad publicity that goes this way: "I don't care what the press says about me so long as it spells my name properly."

Libraries and museums contain fabulous collections from people who do not want their names to disappear from history. College and university campuses have countless buildings named after wealthy donors who want their names perpetuated. American presidents make sure libraries are founded to memorialize their names. Walk into any church and you are likely to see windows donated by people whose names are inscribed there so they won't be forgotten.

Most of us never take the time to remember a stranger's name. But politicians and fund-raisers make recalling names an art form. They know that people enjoy having their names recalled. "To recall a voter's name is statesmanship; to forget it is oblivion."

People resent having their names spoken with scorn or condescension. Lovers expect their names to be used with affection. The insulting use of a name has sometimes led to duels that ended in death. Name-calling among nations has sometimes led to devastating wars.

Some of our most successful magazines built their popularity around people's names. Henry Luce, founder of *Time* magazine, elevated the old journalistic axiom that "Names make news" to a hugely successful technique by putting a newsworthy person—with his name—on each cover of his weekly.

Time became so good at this that it spawned numerous imitations and became as famous as the stars on its covers. Eventually, especially with the annual "Person of the Year" cover, *Time*'s anointing of a cover person has become a secular version of canonization—or demonization if the person is on the world's most hated list.

Salespersons have always known that customers like to be known by name. Memory training to make this possible is a regular part of the orientation of a sales executive.

What's in a name? Shakespeare said that a rose by any other name would still be a rose. That may be true for roses but not for people. Men and women cherish their names and do not want others making fun of them.

Now, just as humans are protective about their names, so is God. The Lord tells Moses that the Second Commandment asks us to respect and reverence God's name. We should not use God's name in an insulting manner, just as we do not want anyone to slur our names. We ought not use God's name to justify cruel, unjust or destructive behavior toward others.

The prophets taught God's covenant people to so reverence the name of God that they should not pronounce it at all. God told Moses at the burning bush that his name is *Yahweh* ("I AM"). As the centuries passed, the people avoided desecrating God's name by using an alternative word, *Adonai,* the Hebrew word for Lord. (It is *Kyrios* in Greek.)

Today, many English-speaking Jews continue this custom, even preferring silence in referring to God's name so they will avoid any irreverence. Some write the holy name as G-d, to maintain the sense of awe that they desire to express.

Hallowed Be Thy Name

When Jesus taught us the Our Father, he asked us first to pray, "Hallowed be thy name." Holy be the name of God. These words invite us to recognize the holiness of God. In the sixth chapter of Isaiah, the prophet has a vision of the glory of God. As he gazes on the magnificent beauty of God, he hears angels sing, "Holy, holy, holy is the Lord" (Isaiah 6:3). The angels teach Isaiah that the vision of love, beauty and purity he beholds is summed up in the word *holy.*

We praise God's holiness in every Mass at the beginning of the Eucharistic Prayer. To sing of God's name as holy is to affirm that God himself is total holiness. Whenever we think of the Second Commandment, we need to hear Christ's prayer about the holiness of God's name. Jesus leads us into the mystery of God's inner life as well as to his loving plan to save us.

At the burning bush, Moses asked God his name. When God replied, "I AM," Moses learned that God is personal. God is not just a star, or the sun and moon, or even a tree. God is a loving personal presence intent on bringing us salvation from sin and the gift of divine life. God's revelation of himself is like a divine ecstasy. God did not want to keep his holy love within, but rather to let it rush out of the heart of divinity into creation and ultimately into salvation. God expressed his love by calling Moses to liberate his people from the slavery of Egypt and promising him full and complete divine support for this difficult mission.

At Sinai, God formed Israel into a holy people. He had made each of them into his own image. They had the capacity to be holy. "You shall be to me a kingdom of priests, a holy nation" (Exodus 19:6).

To Isaiah, God further revealed that he is pure holiness. His name is not only personal but holy. The greatest holy name of God is his Son, Jesus Christ, our Lord and Savior. "At the name of Jesus/every knee should bend,/of those in heaven and on earth and under the earth..." (Philippians 2:10). Jesus wants to celebrate that truth. The Church echoes his teaching:

> The second commandment enjoins respect for the Lord's name.... Respect for his name is an expression of the respect owed to the mystery of God himself and to the whole sacred reality it evokes. The *sense of the sacred* is part of the virtue of religion. (CCC, 2161, 2144)

Life Application

1) Describe some experiences you personally or others have had in which an abuse of a personal name occurred. What resulted from the acts? Were they taken seriously or laughed off? Why do you think our names seem so important to us? Why do people get offended when they are called belittling names? What are we to make of the old rhyme, "Sticks and stones may break my bones, but names will never hurt me"?

2) If you were teaching a child to honor God's name, how would you go about this? How did you learn to reverence the name of God? Who taught you to honor Christ's name? What method did they use? How do

you react when you hear God's name used in a curse, or as a swear word or even a blasphemy?

3) As you reflect on the opening story from *The Mission*, what other kinds of stories could you recall that involve a similar misuse of God's name? What makes people invoke God's name on behalf of a cause that is actually opposed to God's will for our health, happiness and salvation? Whom could you cite as outstanding abusers of God's name? State why you picked them.

• THERE ARE NUMEROUS WAYS TO MAKE WRONG USE OF GOD'S NAME. (CCC, 2147-2155)

O Holy Mountain!

In his *Reader's Digest* article "Which Mountain Did Moses Climb?" Gordon Gaskill describes a pilgrimage to the traditional site of Sinai. On the morning of the climb, he and his traveling companions heard the bell of St. Catherine's monastery pealing out its morning call—33 strokes, one for each year of Jesus' life. The bell awoke people of three faiths. Jewish hikers crawled out of their sleeping bags. Christian pilgrims made coffee. The Moslem guide touched his head to the ground for his first prayer of the day. No other spot, Gaskill declared, so justifies the phrase "out of this world."

The word *sacred* means "set apart." It implies that there is a dignity and sense of worth that requires setting apart in order that the value be recognized and cherished. Gaskill had that feeling about Sinai, an emotion so real that he characterized the mountain as "out of this world."

This feeling for the sacred may be found in many of our experiences. It is the foundation of our appreciation of the sacredness of God and his holy name. It is the reason why we are moved to honor God's name as well as are loath to make wrong use of the divine name, either through casual (or malicious) curses, obscenities or blasphemies. We can also misuse the divine name by invoking it to justify evil behavior against others, as we saw in our opening story about *The Mission.*

> The *sense of the sacred* is part of the virtue of religion....The second commandment *prescribes respect for the Lord's name*...God calls each one by name. Everyone's name is sacred.... It demands respect as the sign of the one who bears it. (CCC, 2144, 2142, 2158)

We treat with respect those we love, and we hold them sacred. We speak their names with affection. Freedom of speech in America is a precious right, but that right is endangered when it is abused and exploited.

It is no secret that the entertainment world—especially movies, plays, novels and popular music—has become coarse, vulgar, uncivilized, blasphemous in thought, word and deed. The sense of the sacred has vanished from most of these productions. The art world, both in photography and painting, is following suit. Even ads are pushing the edges, particularly those for underclothing.

The dialogue in these productions and writings routinely uses the name of Jesus Christ in a casual, disrespectful and unloving way. Frequently the holy name is webbed into a stream of obscenity, vulgarity and raw language. The authors argue this is simply a reflection of how the characters talk in real life.

But one may respond that this is either an excuse for a lack of imagination in their creative process or, worse, a deliberate effort to desacralize the holiness of God. We may further posit that this corruption of language debases the readers, viewers and listeners instead of lifting up their spirits and souls to the noble potential that human dignity deserves. It is certainly contrary to the intent of the Second Commandment:

> The second commandment *forbids the abuse of God's name*, i.e., every improper use of the names of God, Jesus Christ, but also of the Virgin Mary and all the

saints.... Blasphemy is contrary to the respect due God and his holy name.... It is also blasphemous to make use of God's name to cover up criminal practices, to reduce people to servitude, to torture prisoners or put them to death. (CCC, 2146, 2148)

The Holy Name Society

It becomes clearer today why there have been forms of a Holy Name Society for centuries. This society is an association of Catholic laypeople devoted to the promotion of love and reverence for the name of Jesus and God. Its members discourage profanity, obscenity and blasphemies. They are out to clean up language in both a human and a religious sense.

Ours is not the first culture to lapse into the corrosion of talk. The Dominican father Blessed John of Vercelli founded an association dedicated to respecting the holy name around 1250. Even a pope—Gregory X—felt it necessary to support it by adding papal approval at the Council of Lyons in 1274. Despite the great glory of Christendom at the height of medieval life, the scourge of vulgar and blasphemous language was prevalent enough that efforts to purify it occurred at the summit of Church life.

Periodically, the strength of this society declined and there was a new surge of irreverence toward God's name. At various times through the centuries, over 25 popes issued statements of support for the Holy Name Society, endorsing its goals and enriching its members with spiritual benefits.

It became more than an activist group with a special issue. It is now also a community dedicated to the sanctification of its members through retreats, holy hours, devotions and other forms of prayer. While it is normally known as a men's group, it welcomes women as well. In the first half of the twentieth century, the men's groups were visible at enormous rallies and parades that were designed to increase male spirituality and Catholic identity as much as to make men stop cursing, swearing or misusing God's name.

Given the current resurgence of bad language showing up everywhere in most of the media, it may be time for an updated version of the Holy Name Society. The principle to follow is, "Let the good crowd out the bad." When Christian people resolutely honor language as a means to become the best we are meant to be, then a proper counterforce is introduced into society. At the very least, our public delivery systems of language (films, TV, radio, newspapers, magazines, books, the Internet, popular songs) should be invited to clean the stable, and yes, even shamed into doing so.

Allied to this issue are sacrilegious examples of so-called artwork, such as picturing a crucifix immersed in urine, or the Blessed Mother smeared with elephant dung. These scandalous productions should arouse our people of faith to examine the state of reverence for the holy among ourselves.

Art critic Sister Wendy commented on this kind of art by calling it shallow, as being unable to draw people to truth. Its weakness, aside from the corrupting nature of the work, is that it appeals to the most superficial reactions of people and leaves them exactly there—awash on the surface of life, and lacking the capacity to open viewers to the depth that true art is meant to plumb.

By and large the Christophers' motto still needs saying, "Don't curse the darkness; light a candle." This is not meant to excuse us from making critical judgments or mounting passionate protests, but rather to liberate us from energy-draining and time-wasting recriminations. Name the devil and move on.

The positive message of the Second Commandment is this: Value the sacredness of the person, the holiness of God, the sanctity and mystery of life and creation. Love and reverence are synonymous.

We need to encourage a recovery of the sense of the sacred among believers and all people of goodwill. Actually, there are some small hints of a turnaround. Pope John Paul II's meditations *Crossing the Threshold of Hope* has been a best-seller. Angel Records has sold over three million copies of Spanish monks singing Gregorian chant. The president of the Czech Republic, Vaclav Havel, has delivered a speech about his spiritual journey, causing hundreds of people to come forward and share their own experiences.

Attendance at religious retreats has boomed. Gethsemane Abbey in Kentucky and Spencer Abbey in Massachussetts are booked a year ahead. "Now it's suddenly OK to use the S words—soul, sacred, spiritual, sin. A majority of Americans (fifty-eight percent) say they feel the need to experience spiritual growth. And a third of all adults report having had a mystical or religious experience" (*Newsweek* [28 November 1994], 54). As this search for the sacred expands, the due reverence for God, people and the environment will increase.

Life Application

1) Everyone stands for something that is so precious to her that it is considered sacred and not to be disrespected. What are the sacred persons, places and things in your life? (Examples include family members, bedroom, name, religion, job, clothing styles, ethnic origin.) Why is the reality of the sacred so common even in a secular society? If you were to rank the five most sacred realities in your life, what would they be?

2) What do you think about the increase of vulgar, profane, blasphemous language in public entertainment? Why is it happening? How prevalent is the lack of discipline in language within families today? What solutions to the problem have you found appealing and effective?

3) What is your reaction to artwork that treats images of Christ and Mary in a sacrilegious manner? When its proponents argue that their free-speech rights protect them from any censorship, what are we to think? Should tax money be used to fund such art? What are the underlying reasons why this form of expression is taking place? How can we rebuild a civilization of love and respect that would preclude these acts?

• OUR CHRISTIAN NAMING AT BAPTISM CALLS US TO HOLINESS. (CCC, 2156-2159)

The Love You've Known Is Always Yours

An eighty-five-year-old widower went to see a therapist. He wanted to discuss his feelings about having a cancer operation on one lobe of his lung. He had reviewed all his options and finally decided to have the operation. Was there anything he could do to promote healing after the surgery?

He and the therapist discussed exercise, diet and the possibility of Chinese herbs and acupuncture. The therapist wondered how he acquired the strength to go ahead with the operation. He spoke of a daydream he had several weeks before. He had been reading the paper and dozed off.

Then it seemed his wife came in and sat with him. She appeared to be young once more. He was struck by the love in her eyes. His fear eased a little. Then an old friend came into the room and stood behind his wife. The friend's face showed the love that had cemented a lifelong friendship. Then the man's brother appeared beside his friend and also radiated love.

Soon the room was filled with family, friends, teachers, students, children, grandchildren, even the family pets. Eventually there were sixty people. They all reminded him of the value of his life. He was no longer alone. Fear let go of him and he was ready for surgery whether he would survive or not.

"What a beautiful thing," said the therapist.

"Yes," he said, "and most of those people are dead now. I guess anything good you've ever been given is yours forever." He sat there quietly, smiling to himself. (Adapted from *Kitchen Table Wisdom*, Rachel Naomi Remen [New York: Riverhead Books, 1997], 165-166)

The effectiveness of human love, which this story teaches, is a parable of the love of God, which is ours forever. This is particularly true at our Baptism, when God's eyes look on us with affectionate love, a power that transforms us into Christians. God's love enfolds us and eases out whatever fears we may have.

At our Baptisms, we receive our Christian names. This confirms God's love for us and plants in us our call to holiness. The *Catechism* teaches that our responsiveness to this call will help us avoid tampering with the holy name of God. When we share in God's holiness, we will not be inclined to curse, swear or blaspheme. Lovers venerate each other. When we grow in love for God, we spontaneously honor God's name.

Our means to holiness are prayer, worship, love for others and service to their needs. In daily prayer, we commune with God, learn to be his friend, accept the love he offers. Prayer deepens our outlook on life and moves us away from whatever would separate us from God.

> The Christian begins his day, his prayers and his activities with the Sign of the Cross: "in the name of the Father and of the Son and of the Holy Spirit. Amen." The baptized person dedicates the day to the glory of God and calls on the Savior's grace which lets him act in the Spirit as a child of the Father. (*CCC*, 2157)

This has not always been easy in a culture that prizes the privatization of religion. We are all familiar with the various ways that cultural movements press the separation of church and state. The idea is that faith ought to be a personal matter conducted on private time. Public affairs should be conducted without benefit of religious affiliation, church symbols or any effort to influence public policy from a faith-based point of view.

Father Richard John Neuhaus calls this phenomenon "the naked public square," an external forum where there is a blackout on God and religion. Court cases about eliminating prayer from public school classrooms, graduations and football games are well known and symptomatic of the ascendancy of the secular in public culture. The result of this is a false division between faith and life, and also a loss of communal support for prayer and faith growth.

Oddly, God's name has been largely banished from our public institutions, but our cultural ones are allowed to bandy it about in all kinds of scandalous ways. Laws are enacted to keep God's name out of schools and to protect the entertainment industry in using the Lord's name as much as it likes in curses, blasphemies and other demeaning manners.

But there has been a countercultural movement growing that welcomes the return of prayer and Bible reflection in places other than the family hearth or the local church. It has gained access to public awareness under the all-embracing title of spirituality. People are suddenly becoming open about their spirituality. The Gallup Organization reports that forty-eight percent of people admit they have talked about their religion in the workplace on a given day.

The widely read magazine *Business Week* ran a cover story, "Religion in the Workplace," in which the author explored the growing presence of spirituality in corporate America.

> Does modern life leave you too busy to enjoy God or pray as you like? 51% of Americans say yes.
>
> Across the country, major league executives are meeting for prayer breakfasts and spiritual conferences.... In Minneapolis, 150 business chiefs lunch monthly at a private, ivy-draped club to hear other chief executives draw business solutions from the

Bible.... In Boston, heavy hitters such as retired Raytheon chairman, Thomas L. Phillips, meet at an invitation-only prayer breakfast, called First Tuesday. There are 10,000 Bible and prayer groups in workplaces that meet regularly, according to the Fellowship for Companies for Christ International. Just five years ago there was only one conference on spirituality and the workplace; now there are over 30. (*Business Week* [1 November 1999], 152-3)

This development is not without its problems. Sectarian conflicts cause tensions. How are bosses going to resolve competing forms of religion, whether Christian, Jewish, Hindu, Moslem or Buddhist? From all reports, they are generally doing well. One thing on their side is that the new movement of prayer in the workplace is helping productivity and retention of the workforce, especially in the fast-food industries. Despite problems, the new movement rolls on and appears to be here for the long run, and presumably is not just another fad.

Imperfect it may be, but it is still a healthy sign for a society that has prized openness in everything except religion. Psychology tells us, "We are as sick as our secrets." When religious faith is supposed to be a secret in a free society, it is not out of place to wonder out loud about whether this is healthy for us. The surge of spirituality that is being reported can help us all get in touch with our souls, an experience that leads us to regain relationships with God.

So far no report has been made about the effect of this new spirituality movement on the quality of language in the workplace. Has it been able to reduce profanity, blasphemy, dirty jokes and other coarse forms of conversation? Has it had an impact on preventing the wrong use of God's name? One can only guess. It is not too unreasonable to surmise that a living spirituality that moves a person closer to God would have a positive impact on how a person uses God's name. If I love someone, I am not likely to use that person's name in a disrespectful manner.

Some Prayer Guidance

When God names us at Baptism, he calls us to prayer, which is another way of saying God invites us to a lifelong love conversation with him. The prayer conversation begins with God. The push to pray comes from God, not from us. That is what Saint Augustine meant when he wrote, "Late have I loved you, O Lord, O Beauty ever ancient, ever new." He attributes to God the graces that made this possible for him.

Prayerful people will honor God's name because they love the God whose name they revere. There is a special reason why Scripture associates prayer with the action of the heart, for the heart is the seat of love. Scripture connects prayer with the heart over one thousand times. Saint Thérèse says simply, "Prayer is a surge of the heart."

We tend to forget God who sustains our life and never stops loving us. The philosopher Heidegger says that the greatest human failing is "forgetfulness of being." We can restate this to say that forgetfulness of God is a weakness that ever confronts us. The biblical prophets are always urging us to remember God's presence. They use the expression "memory of the heart" to awaken us to this call.

Saint Paul tells us that we should "pray always" (1 Thessalonians 5:17). But we cannot pray always if we do not pray every day at specific times. We must consciously will to pray. Knowing this need of ours, the Church proposes prayer times, such as morning and evening prayer, grace before and after meals, the Sunday Eucharist, the Liturgy of the Hours. The cycle of liturgical seasons— Advent, Lent, Pentecost—and the feasts of Our Lady and the saints are other ways to help us get a prayer rhythm in our lives.

There is a small prayer that reminds us of the types of prayer to which we are called by our baptismal naming: "May the Lord be in my mind, my lips and my heart." These words are accompanied by making a little sign of the cross with our thumbs on our forehead, lips and heart. They correspond to vocal, mental and contemplative prayer.

Vocal Prayer

Vocal prayer is essential. The apostles were impressed with Christ's silent prayer. They asked him to teach them to pray. He taught them a vocal prayer, the Our Father. Jesus prayed aloud the psalms and hymns of the synagogue. He publicly praised God for his graces and vocally prayed in anguish at Gethsemane.

We need to pray externally to express the internal movements of our feelings. We are not pure souls but an integration of body and spirit. Vocal prayer suits our natures. Naturally, our hearts must be in our words. It is not the number of words we speak so much as the interior fervor we bring to these words.

Meditation

In meditation, we struggle to probe the meaning and purpose of the Christian life. This requires concentration and inner attentiveness. This is not easy. In most cases, we use books to help us sustain our search: the Bible, writings of the fathers, texts by spiritual writers. We also can be helped by the "book" of creation and history through which God seeks to touch us.

To meditate on what we read brings us to reflect on ourselves in the light of the thoughts and challenges before us. We are drawn to figure out what God wants of us. Spiritual masters have proposed a great variety of methods for meditation. Find the one that suits you. Learn how to let the Spirit guide you to Jesus.

Meditation organizes our full personal attention, using our minds, feelings, imagination, intuition and desire. The Church urges us to meditate on the mysteries of Christ as seen in Scripture, liturgy and the rosary. A living, conscious and active union with Jesus is the goal.

Contemplation

In contemplative prayer, we rest directly in Jesus. Saint Teresa of Avila says that "it means taking time frequently to be alone with him who we know loves us." Like all prayer, this demands time from us. The guiding principle is, give God the time, and he will give you the time.

In contemplation, we really become the children that Jesus urged upon his disciples. We come to Christ with the simplicity and directness of which a child is capable, but without the naiveté, because we bring the capacity of an adult with a treasury of life experiences. In this kind of prayer above all, we become conscious of the "gift" of prayer, for we cannot engineer or produce it at will. We begin to appreciate what covenant means.

The Curé of Ars said that in front of the Blessed Sacrament, "I look at Jesus and he looks at me." Contemplation is a gaze of faith on the mystery of God. When Jesus looks at us, he purifies our minds from inadequate understandings of his hopes for us, cleanses our desires from wanting anything but him, opens our hearts to him alone. In this silent love, we journey through the death and resurrection of Christ in ever deeper ways.

This is the spiritual transformation that our baptismal naming implies. Because of it, we would never dream of dishonoring the name of God.

Life Application

1) How often do you think of your baptismal name? How do you communicate with your patron saint? Why do we say that baptismal naming is a call to holiness? Why would a proper understanding of this help us acquire a reverence for God's holy name? How often have you been challenged to develop a lifestyle that leads you to

spiritual transformation in Christ? If it were offered to you, how do you think you would respond?

2) How have you experienced the impact of privatized religion in our American culture? We can support a proper understanding of the separation of church and state but not a separation of faith and culture. What would this mean to you? How should our Catholic faith be brought to bear on public life? How do you react to the disrespectful use of God's name in our entertainment industry?

3) Why is a regular prayer life a necessary part of maintaining a reverence for God's name? In reviewing the forms of vocal prayer, where would you see you need improvement in your own prayer life? How often do you practice meditation? How would you respond to the invitation to spend 15 to 30 minutes a day in meditation? In what way could you see yourself drawn to contemplative prayer?

Meditation

Solomon once wrote that the fool believes everything. The community of fools was shocked because now everyone will recognize who is a fool, and this is a dangerous situation. So they convened a world congress and debated the problem a long time. They decided to take another position: The fool doesn't believe anything.

Their conclusion shows us that nothing has changed. The fact that fools believe everything doesn't show the folly of belief, but rather the folly of indiscrimination. The same thing is true of their new motto, not believing anything. What power of discrimination do you have when you say that the less you believe the wiser you are?

Some people may say love makes the world go round. I think faith makes the world go round. Sometimes the faith is the wrong one, but faith is the moving power of most things that happen. History shows this again and again. The biggest changes were made by faith. (Rabbi Adin Steinsaltz, *The Washington Post* [21 April 1988])

Prayer

Blessed be your holy name, O God, Father, Son and Holy Spirit. Your love for us moves us to honor your name. We are saddened and appalled by the desecration of your divine name in our culture. We resolve through prayer and reparation to restore the dignity of your name in our society as well as in our own personal lives. We ask for the graces of spiritual transformation so that we may have the wisdom to know and do what is best in this matter. Adorable Trinity, we worship you and honor you with our whole being. AMEN.

O Lord, our Lord, How awesome is your name through all the earth! (Psalm 8:1)

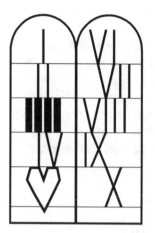

Third Commandment

Love God's Sabbath

Take care to keep holy the sabbath day.... The sabbath was made for man, not man for the sabbath....[so] the Son of Man is Lord, even of the sabbath.

—DEUTERONOMY 5:12A; MARK 2:27-28

Rediscovering the Christian Sabbath

For many baby-boom generation Catholics like Catherine Dillon, childhood memories of going to Mass are as vivid as the powder-blue cover on the *Baltimore Catechism*. She will never forget how her mother seemed transfixed at the consecration of the bread and wine: "She didn't even blink." And she can hear as if it were yesterday the words of her father, when any of his children expressed doubts about getting out of bed for morning Mass: "There are people who live where they're not allowed to worship. You should consider yourself fortunate." They did. They still do.

For Dillon, thirty-nine, the celebration of the Mass remains the center of her spiritual life. "It gives a sense of calm to my day, to my week," she says. "There can be ups and downs in other aspects of my life, but the Mass is one of the constants." (*U.S. News*

Catherine Dillon's parents also taught her that going to Mass should have a practical side. Her parents participated in the Birthright movement, opening their home to unmarried pregnant teenagers for a few weeks or months. Catherine herself tutors young people in their religion and works at a soup kitchen in her parish.

Christ's Eucharistic Body is both bread for the soul and bread for the world.

Do You Love God's Sabbath?

The Catechism shows us ways to do this:

- Honor the Lord's Day as a day of rest (page 50).

- Understand why Sunday Eucharist is essential (page 56).

- Participate more fully in the Eucharist (page 63).

• HONOR THE LORD'S DAY AS A DAY OF REST.
(CCC, 2168-2173; 2184-2188)

> "Remember the sabbath day, to keep it holy. Six days you shall labor and do all your work; but the seventh day is a sabbath to the Lord your God; in it you shall not do any work..." (Exodus 20:8-10; see also Deuteronomy 5:12-15). We honor this commandment by resting from our ordinary labors and worshiping God. (CCC, 2168)

Many people in contemporary society do not need much urging to take a day off on Sunday. They do not necessarily do so for religious reasons.

Sociologist J. Russell Hale calls the new leisure seekers in American society the "happy hedonists." Whether they are retirees in Sun City or surfers in San Clemente, their comments sound the same.

A young bachelor says, "Surfing was great this morning. Now I'm driving up to the mountains to ski. Church can't compete with this."

"We were slaves to the clock for forty years," the retiree says. "Now we're free for peace, serenity and the good life. We have plenty to make us happy—swimming, fishing, walking, art classes, sculpture and music, gardening clubs, folk-dancing and cooking. Churches must have something distinctive to offer to engage us."

The employed happy hedonist says, "I work six days. I save the seventh for recreation. Church can't compete with boating, bicycling, mountain climbing, skiing, aerobic dancing. When it comes to priorities, I come first. If I can't be happy, there is no way I can make others happy."

In one sense, the happy hedonist hews closely to the invitation of the Third Commandment. God said, "I worked six days. I'm going to rest on the seventh."

Rest from one's labors, and personal renewal are gifts of the Third Commandment.

Everyone needs a break from routine to refresh body, soul and mind. Studies on the destructive effects of stress properly motivate people to seek essential relaxation. Henry Ford once said that it is not only good religion but also good business not to work on the Sabbath. He said that his company would have had the famous Model A car in production six months earlier had he forbidden his engineers to work on Sunday. Fatigue set in during the frantic effort to meet production deadlines: "It took us all week to straighten out the mistakes that were made on the day we should have rested."

Biblical Teaching About the Sabbath Rest

The Third Commandment invites us to take our minds off everyday concerns and open ourselves to relaxing occupations. In contemporary terms, it says, "Take time each week for personal renewal." The biblical words also urge us to use Sabbath rest to renew and deepen our covenant relationship with God.

In Exodus 20:8-11, the Third Commandment stresses the rest aspect of the Sabbath, recalling God's rest at the conclusion of creation. Deuteronomy 5:12 approaches the issue by calling us to remember our covenant love engagement to God.

In biblical teaching, the religious meaning of the Sabbath embraces both creation and covenant, two major events in the salvation of the world. Civilizations other than that of the Hebrews had Sabbaths, days on which work was taboo. But to Israel, the Sabbath was a tithing of time, a day consecrated to God. Just as one tithed the firstborn of the flock or the firstfruits of a harvest, so one tithed work time.

Deuteronomy 5:14 calls attention to the social aspects of Sabbath: "No work may be done then, whether by you, or your son or daughter, or your male or female slave, or your ox or ass or any of your beasts...." The next verse calls for remembrance of Israel's enslavement in Egypt and God's covenant deliverance. "That is why the LORD, your God, has commanded you to observe the sabbath day" (Deuteronomy 5:15).

Exodus 20:11 gives us the "creation reason" for Sabbath observance: "In six days the LORD made the heavens and the earth, the sea and all that is in them; but on the seventh day he rested. That is why the LORD has blessed the sabbath day and made it holy." Exodus 31:12-17 elaborates on this connection between creation and the sabbath.

The idea that God rests on the sabbath is an expression of biblical faith. Creation is the first act in the history of salvation. Once the work of creation was over, God began his historical love affair with all men and women. If all we do is work, not only shall we have no time to play and relax, we won't have any time to love. God, too, takes time off from work, not just to rest but to nurture us in divine love.

The biblical history of sabbath observance demonstrates that it was a day for joy and celebration. "Then [on the sabbath] you shall delight in the LORD,/ and I will make you ride on the heights of the earth..." (Isaiah 58:14). Everyone was to *enjoy* a day off. Worship was part of the renewal process. At liturgy the people looked back to their roots, praised and thanked God for his love and renewed their covenant faith. They considered the whole day holy because it reminded them of God's gifts: creation and God's loving attentiveness to them in their history.

As the centuries passed, numerous burdensome rules were added to Sabbath observance. The *Book of Jubilees*, a useful sourcebook of Old Testament Jewish customs, forbids the marital act, lighting a fire or preparing food on this day. The *Mishna* (a rabbinic commentary on biblical observance) lists 39 kinds of work forbidden on the Sabbath. In New Testament times, the Pharisees forbade people to carry a bed (see John 5:10), to heal a sick person (see Mark 3:2) or to pick a few ears of corn (see Matthew 12:2) on the Sabbath.

Jesus rejected this restrictive view of the Sabbath. He preached that love and concern for people was more important than these joyless rules. "The sabbath was made for man, not man for the sabbath," he insisted (Mark 2:27), and claimed that "...the Son of Man is lord even of the Sabbath" (Mark 2:28).

Scripture teaches that the Sabbath is a time to rest, relax, enjoy God and one another. It is a day for reflecting on creation, the Creator and the love covenant we have with God.

Sabbath Rest Is Needed Today

In the early days of the Industrial Revolution, we heard about sweatshops in our big cities where men, women and children worked 15 hours a day, sometimes 7 days a week, in horrible and unsafe workplaces for slave wages. Of the money made, eighty percent was spent on food—most of it bread and potatoes, once in a while a cabbage. There was no health care or the possibility of saving money and buying a home.

Today those sweatshops have returned to cities like

New York, Miami and Los Angeles. In New York alone, 2,000 sweatshops employ 60,000 people. A forty-four-year-old immigrant works 12 hours a day, 7 days a week, in a windowless garment shop, earning $200.00 in a good week—less than $2.50 an hour. The fire exits are sealed shut by metal gates with large padlocks. The owners pay in cash, deny the workers minimum wage, holidays or overtime compensation.

These thousands of workers get no Sundays off, no days off at all. Fines are cheap and federal supervisors and fire inspectors are so overworked they cannot keep up with all the violations.

The point of this story is not only the terrible social injustice to these unfortunate people. It is also the denial of regular time off for them to regain their strength and renew their human dignity. Most of them are helpless to defend themselves, unable to speak English and terrified of deportation. They deserve a living wage for their families and time to restore their health. Their employers deny them a Sabbath rest as well as other benefits.

But millions of people in our culture freely deny themselves a Sabbath rest, time for rest and relaxation. The workaholism so characteristic of a consumer society means that Sunday is rarely a day of rest. Obviously, there are people who need to work for the public good on the Sabbath—police, firefighters, water monitors and so on. Still, there is a growing number of businesspeople in the service sector who have decided to close on Sundays.

The *Catechism* maintains the scriptural call for Sabbath rest:

> God's action is the model for human action. If God "rested and was refreshed" on the seventh day, man, too ought to "rest" and should let others, especially the poor, "be refreshed." The sabbath brings everyday work to a halt and provides a respite. It is a day of protest against the servitude of work and the worship of money. (CCC, 2172)

In his book *Waiting for the Weekend*, Canadian author Witold Rybczynski says a cultural shift has taken place in North America: "Where once the week consisted of weekdays and Sunday, now it is weekdays and the weekend. Ask most people to name the first day of the week and they will answer, 'Monday, of course'; fifty years ago, the answer would have been Sunday" (New York: Penguin USA, 1992).

For some, the weekend is busier and more exhausting than workdays. For them, Sunday is neither a day of rest nor a day for worship.

The wisdom of the Third Commandment is that life should be a rhythm of work and rest. Without a work break, we become a stressed-out society with all the well-known tension-related diseases, especially heart trouble, our biggest killer.

God made us and knows what is best for our human development. While God cannot grow tired and needs no rest in the strict sense of the word, even God "rested" on the seventh day to give us the example (cf. Genesis 2:2).

Our weekly day off should give us perspective on the meaning and value of what we do and help us see our lives against the backdrop of a bigger picture. It is a day for looking at creation—and the Creator from whom all these blessings flow.

It is a day for more relaxed time with family and friends, a day for reading and cultural activities, a day for leisure in the fullest sense of that word. From this viewpoint, the Third Commandment is part of our "health plan," the breather that restores our vitality. It is also essential for our spirituality and its eucharistic dimension.

Life Application

1) What is your usual Sunday routine? How could your weekends be more restful and personally renewing? Why have weekends become as frantic as the workweek? How do some families you know of manage to resist the

tide of busyness and make Sunday and the weekend restful and creative interludes? What is the secret of their success?

2) How would you explain to others the scriptural teaching about Sabbath rest? Why is Sabbath observance said to be a good time to reflect on creation, the Creator and the covenant? Why does tithing of time to God seem like a good idea? Why did Jesus object to the accumulation of dozens of little rules for keeping the Sabbath rest since he obviously favored the basic call to rest from labor?

3) Throughout history, the Church has insisted on preserving the Sabbath rest, especially on behalf of the poor workers whose bosses gave them no time off. What are examples of this injustice today that you know of personally? We know the health benefits of taking a break. What are some of the spiritual benefits?

- **UNDERSTAND WHY SUNDAY EUCHARIST IS ESSENTIAL.** (*CCC*, 2174-2179)

I Heard the Bell for Mass

Last week God tested my faithfulness to him. I had just arrived at our new position in the desert. Each of us had to dig our fighting holes. My platoon sergeant came and said, "Sunday Mass is at 5 p.m." I thanked him. I was tired but I still wanted to go to Mass. About 4:45 p.m. it started to rain pretty bad. The wind made it more uncomfortable. Then I heard the bell for Mass.

"Well," I said to myself, "this is a test of your faithfulness to God." Then the devil said to me, "If you go out there, you are going to get all wet and you will be miserable." I grabbed my hat and headed for Mass. After Mass, I was wet and cold, and had no dry clothes to change into. See, I thought about this and said, "If God sacrificed his body for me, I shouldn't mind getting wet at all." (From a letter from a soldier in the Persian Gulf War)

This good and faithful soldier maintained his faith in the call of God to observe the Sabbath by participating in the Sunday Eucharist. We have seen the importance of Sabbath rest. Now we must examine the nature and necessity of sabbath worship.

From the time of the apostles, the Church has celebrated the Eucharist every seventh day, which is called the Lord's Day, or Sunday. Christianity moved the Sabbath observance from Saturday to Sunday because this was the day Jesus rose from the dead. The day of Christ's Resurrection is the first day of the week and remembers the first day of creation. The apostles designated the celebration of the Lord's Supper as the center of Sunday worship, where the whole community of faith may encounter the risen Lord who invites them to this heavenly banquet.

> The celebration of Sunday observes the moral commandment inscribed by nature in the human heart to render to God an outward, visible, public and regular worship "as a sign of his universal beneficence to all." Sunday worship fulfills the moral command of the Old Covenant, taking up its rhythm and spirit in weekly celebration of the Creator and Redeemer of his people. (*CCC*, 2176)

Sunday Eucharist celebrates the Passover of Jesus Christ, which brings to fulfillment the hopes and expectations of the original Passover.

In the first Covenant, the people offered a sacrifice of bread and wine to thank God for the wheat and grape harvests. The Exodus experience brought new meaning to these rituals. The unleavened bread that Israel eats every year at Passover recalls their hasty departure from Egypt. The memory of manna bread in the desert testifies that Israel lives by the bread of God's Word. The "cup of blessing" at the end of the Jewish Passover meal expresses the wine of joy that God will remain faithful to his people.

Jesus gave new meaning to the blessing of the bread and the cup. In his bread miracle, when Jesus blessed, broke and distributed the loaves through his disciples to feed the crowds, he prefigured the magnificent abundance of the unique bread of his Eucharist. When he changed water into wine at Cana, he revealed his glory and the kingdom where the faithful will drink the new wine that has become his Blood.

When Jesus first taught the mystery of the Eucharist, he faced resistance. "This saying is hard; who can accept it?" (John 6:60). The same thing happened each time he announced his forthcoming cross. The cross and the Eucharist are stumbling blocks that divide believers from unbelievers. "So you also want to leave?" (John 6:67). Jesus asks this question in every historical period. He calls us to a faith that understands that in receiving the Eucharist we receive him.

At the Last Supper, Jesus gave the Passover meal its new and definitive meaning. The supper anticipated Christ's "passing over" to the Father by his death and resurrection. He is the New Passover celebrated in the Eucharist at the Last Supper.

Jesus commanded his apostles to repeat his words and actions of the Last Supper "until he comes" again in final glory to judge the world and bring the elect to the heavenly banquet where they will be seated at the table of God's kingdom. The Church has been faithful to his command from the very beginning. "They devoted themselves to the teaching of the apostles and to the communal life, to the breaking of bread and to the prayers...Every day they devoted themselves to meeting together in the temple and to breaking bread in their homes. They ate their meals with exultation and sincerity of heart" (Acts 2:42–46). It was above all on "the first day of the week," Sunday, the day of Jesus' Resurrection, that the Christians met "to break bread" (Acts 20:7). And the Church has been doing this ever since in every part of the world.

By Christ's teaching, command and Church Tradition, the Christian Sunday Eucharist has been at the very heart of divine worship in which all members are expected to participate actively. The Eucharist is the source and summit of all the graces needed for Christian spirituality. In this Eucharist is found all the treasures of the Church, which is Christ himself. No greater way exists for observing the worship dimension of the Third Commandment than a living, active and conscious participation in the Mass.

The Church asks us to take part of the Christian Sunday (which includes Saturday evening) and devote it to active participation in the Eucharist. The Church does not confine Sabbath observance to the Mass, but seriously invites us to make eucharistic worship an essential part of that observance. In the eucharistic celebration, we open up our lives to the healing, reconciling and saving love of Christ. Just as rest and relaxation renew our bodies and emotions, so Christ's sacrificial love renews our whole being and shapes our minds and hearts to his values.

Vatican II on the Eucharist

Vatican II's inspiring teaching about the Eucharist merits our attention at this point:

> At the Last Supper, on the night he was betrayed, our Savior instituted the eucharistic sacrifice of his Body and Blood. This he did in order to perpetuate the sacrifice of the Cross throughout the ages until he should come again, and so to entrust to his beloved spouse, the Church, a memorial of his death and resurrection: a sacrament of love, a sign of unity, a bond of charity, a paschal banquet in which Christ is consumed, the mind is filled with grace and a pledge of future glory is given to us.
>
> The Church, therefore, earnestly desires that Christ's faithful, when present at this mystery of faith, should not be there as strangers or silent spectators.

On the contrary, through a good understanding of the rites and prayers they should participate knowingly, devoutly and actively.... Offering the Immaculate Victim, not only through the hands of the priest, but also with him, they should learn to offer themselves too. Through Christ the Mediator they should be drawn day by day into ever closer union with God and each other, so that finally God may be all in all. (*Constitution on the Liturgy*, 47-48)

Hence Eucharist is not meant to be a passive experience of a clerical and choral performance, but an active event in which we selflessly pour out our love to God and to the members of the worshiping community. The more we concentrate on what we bring to it, the more we worship in spirit and truth.

Babette's Feast

Isak Dinesen's lovely short story "Babette's Feast" (in *Anecdotes of Destiny* [New York: Vintage Books, 1993]), which has been made into an award-winning film, illustrates the spiritual attitude we should bring to the worship side of our keeping holy the Sabbath day. The setting is a remote fishing village on the rocky coast of nineteenth-century Denmark. The narrative centers on the lives of Martine and Phillipa, daughters of a devout Lutheran pastor who founded a small sect. The two sisters rejected marriage and chose to continue their father's religious work after his death. Reared to live simply, they live out their lives performing good works for the inhabitants of their tiny fishing village.

They have welcomed Babette, a Parisian refugee from the civil war of 1871, into their home. Babette cooks and keeps house for the sisters in return for room and board and watches the 12 aging members of the sect become increasingly querulous as the years pass. More and more they remember old slights and drift away from the kindly teachings of their founder.

One day Babette receives news from Paris that she has won 10,000 francs in the lottery. She asks Martine and Phillipa if she can use the prize money to prepare a feast for the sect's celebration of the hundredth anniversary of its founder's birth.

The sisters agree, but they are dismayed when the supplies for the feast arrive from Paris: cases of wine and champagne, a live turtle for the soup, live pheasants for the entrée. Wine has scarcely ever passed their lips, and turtle soup sounds like a broth for a "witches' sabbath." They confide their misgivings to the sect, and all decide to partake in the feast but make no comment about it—a silent protest of disapproval.

The guests may have vowed not to speak of the food, but they are warmed by the candlelight, the wine, the superbly prepared food. They begin to talk animatedly, especially recalling the deeds and words of their founder. The good cheer that prevails moves them to repent of recent bad moods and words; they look on one another with fresh kindness and embrace each other with affection:

> They only knew that the rooms had been filled with a heavenly light, as if a small number of halos had blended into one glorious radiance. Taciturn old people received the gift of tongues; ears that for years had been almost deaf were opened to it. Time itself had merged into eternity. Long after midnight the windows of the house shone like gold, and golden song flowed out into the winter air....
>
> The vain illusions of this earth had dissolved before their eyes like smoke, and they saw the universe as it really is. They had been given one hour of the millennium.

When the guests were gone, the sisters went to thank Babette, the only one who had not participated in the feast. They found her amid the greasy pots and pans, totally emptied and exhausted. To their astonishment, they discover she has spent all the prize money on the feast. She will be poor, they tell her. "A great artist, mesdames, is never poor," she replies. Phillipa embraces her and says, "In paradise you will be the great artist that God meant you to be. Ah, how you will enchant the angels!"

Babette's feast is a symbolic liturgy: Babette is the sacrificing hostess for the community of 12. The guests fondly remember the teaching and presence of their founder, and the experience lifts them out of the everyday into the world of transcendence. This story evokes the mystery and meaning of the Lord's Supper, the Eucharist.

It is no secret that participation in the weekly Eucharist has declined in recent decades. Still, the focal point of Catholic religious life is, without a doubt, the weekly Eucharist. Mass attendance is important as a time to praise the Lord for his loving salvation, and an *essential* part of keeping the Sabbath holy.

Growing in Faith

1) How would you describe your lifelong history of participating in Sunday Mass? What people have been influential in shaping your attitudes and practices of Sunday Eucharist participation? How deeply have you examined your personal responsibility for Sunday Mass observance? As you reflect on the Third Commandment and the teachings of Jesus, what impact might this have on your vision of the value of Sunday Eucharist?

2) When you think back on your First Communion, what memories come to your mind? What would you say is different from that day and now regarding your appreciation of the Eucharist? When you read our reflection on the links between the Jewish Passover and the Last Supper, how might that help you see the Mass in a new light?

3) If the Eucharist is the greatest source for our Christian

spirituality, what does that suggest for your present capacity to be involved in the Mass? Why did the apostles, and the Church ever since, choose the Eucharist as the form for Sunday worship? When we speak of the Eucharist as the sacrament of salvation, what are we saying?

• **PARTICIPATE MORE FULLY IN THE EUCHARIST.** (*CCC*, 2180-2183)

Love and Live the Eucharist

We fulfill our worship obligation by participating in the Eucharist either on Sunday or a holy day of obligation (or on the evening before). "On Sundays and other holy days of obligation, the faithful are bound to participate in the Mass.... The Sunday Eucharist is the foundation and confirmation of all Christian practice" (*CCC*, 2180-2181).

We should view the Third Commandment's obligation more as a privilege and joy than simply as a law. When we love the Mass, we do not think of it in terms of burden or obligation. Love moves to the beloved with "light wings," not with leaden feet.

The best way to love the Mass is to live the Mass. Consider the four steps in the prayers of consecration of the bread and wine, which repeat what Jesus did at the Last Supper. There Jesus *takes, blesses, breaks* and *gives* the bread transformed into his Body and the wine changed into his Blood.

Jesus lived those actions on Holy Thursday and most vividly on Good Friday:

- He surrendered himself to his Father, who *takes* him like a shepherd takes a lamb from the flock.

- Then the Father consecrates him, *blesses* him for the coming sacrifice of the cross.

- After this, the Father releases him to be *offered* as a

sacrifice on the cross.

• Lastly, the Father *gives* Jesus to the world as the Bread of Life.

Jesus freely allows himself to be taken. Had he so willed, he could have called on "legions of angels" to save him. He bows before the Father and accepts his consecration to mission. Jesus offers his whole being and body to be offered sacrificially on the cross. Jesus becomes the Living Bread, "baked in the fire of suffering and death," given for the life of the world.

This is the four-step eucharistic model that we can follow in order to put Sabbath worship at the center of our lives. In Mass after Mass, we have the opportunity to be taken by God for Christian service. We can surrender in joy to the Father's will. We may identify with the words of the Mass that beg the Holy Spirit to come and bless and change both the bread and wine in its divine fire—and us as well. We also need the blessing fire of the Spirit to give us the divine way of seeing the world and prepare us for a life of sacrificial love. Like the bread and wine we need spiritual transformation.

We offer our bodies to be a living sacrifice (cf. Romans 12:1), our personhood to be placed at the service of total love of God and neighbor with all the crosses this will entail. Finally, we exult in the knowledge that we can now be "given" to the world as the bread of love, justice and mercy for others.

Here is a prayer you may find helpful:

O Jesus, take my eyes that I may see the world as you did, as a good shepherd full of concern for others. Jesus take my ears, that I may listen to others' needs with a willingness to help them. Take my mouth and fill it with your wisdom so that my words may be a light for others' lives. Jesus take my hands and fill them with your creativity and healing. Take my heart that it may beat with

*Jesus' love and Jesus' mercy for all people. Take my feet
that wherever I walk I may bring your gospel of peace
and a sense of your divine presence.* AMEN.

How can our participation in the Holy Eucharist be made
more effective? Try these suggestions:

Life Application

1) Obtain a Sunday Missal for the purpose of meditating
on the readings before you go to Mass. Everywhere else
in life people get ready for meetings by reading over the
agenda and related materials beforehand. We should do
the same for Mass. If we arrive at Mass with some
prayerful knowledge about the readings, the theme of
the Sunday and the mood of the liturgical season, we
will bring a faith-filled understanding to the liturgy.
Our minds will be open to what God wants to say to us
at Mass.

2) Arrive at Mass with an attitude of giving oneself to the
celebration. Come with ears open to God's word, eyes
open to the beauty of the ritual, throat wide open to
sing and pray with all your strength, and heart to give
God lots of love and praise. Some come to Mass and
complain, "I get nothing out of it." But we only get
what we give. If at the end of Mass we can say, "I loved
and praised God with all my mind, heart and voice,"
then we will find Mass more rewarding.

3) Open yourself to the spirit of community at Mass. The
Eucharist is not for loners. At the Last Supper, the one
loner was Judas, the secret agent at the table. He had
made his private arrangements for the betrayal of Jesus.
He never understood how to be a part of the apostolic
community. Sadly, Jesus let Judas go from the Lord's
Supper. But Judas had already exiled himself internally.
Jesus permitted what Judas had done to himself.

The Eucharist is an agape, a love feast. True love requires a relationship with others. We know the Mass is a sacrifice. Entering the eucharistic community demands a sacrifice from us. The trade-off is satisfying, for only in self-sacrifice does true self-fulfillment occur.

4) Come to Mass with a soul full of prayer. The more deeply we have learned how to pray always, morning, noon and night, the more the Mass will be a joy for us, for the Eucharist is the summit of prayer. The Eucharist perfects, completes and energizes our prayer so that our journey with Jesus becomes ever more intimate throughout our lives.

These four commonsense guidelines can make all the difference in our participation in Sunday Eucharist. They turn a law into love, a burden into a sweet experience, a mystery into an hour of light at the beginning—indeed the center— of our week.

Life in the Spirit

The following checklist addresses some issues related to your Sabbath worship. Use Y for yes, N for No.

___ I generally prepare myself for Sunday Mass.

___ I can see why Mass is the best way to worship God on Sunday.

___ I do not understand how the Last Supper is connected to the Jewish Passover.

___ For me the best part of Mass is Communion.

___ At Eucharist I expect a good homily.

___ I don't know how to apply to my life the consecration words: take, bless, break, give.

___ I believe that by the power of the Spirit and the words of the priest at the consecration, the bread and wine really become the Body and Blood of Jesus Christ.

___ As I grow older I find my desire for regular Sunday worship increases.

___ I like worshiping together with others.

___ I would rather worship God alone in a quiet place amid the beauties of nature.

The above checklist is meant to generate your self-examination regarding God's call for Sabbath worship. You may also like to use these issues as points for a discussion group.

Meditation

Cardinal Francis Xavier Thuan was named archbishop of Saigon just before it fell to the communists. Within a few months, he was arrested and pressured to abandon Catholicism. Because he refused, he was imprisoned for the next 13 years, 9 of which were in solitary confinement.

The only humans he saw were his guards, who were forbidden to speak to him. As he reflected on his condition, he reaffirmed his faith in God and resolved that he would practice fraternal love to his persecutors, especially his guards. Jesus had counseled his disciples to love one's enemies and pray for those who persecute you.

Thuan persevered in loving his enemies and in time found they responded positively, finding his unflagging love irresistible. Once he had made friends with them, he asked them to lend him a knife and give him a piece of wood and some wire. Despite rules against this, they gave him what he asked. He cut a cross out of the wood. He also cut a piece of soap in half and hid the cross in the soap to hide it from the supervisors. He made a chain out of the wire.

He then asked his guards to let his friends send him a little wine each month to soothe his stomach. Again permission was given, and his friends also enclosed some hosts. Each day thereafter, for nine years, Thuan put three drops of wine and one drop of water in the palm of his hand along with a tiny piece of the host. In this way he celebrated Mass, using his memory for the words of institution and the prayers and Gospel stories.

He later said that the Eucharist sustained him with hope and joy all those years. After his release from prison, Archbishop Thuan was assigned by the Vatican to oversee the office for peace and justice. Commenting on his new post, he said, "I like being with people who need reconciliation, since I was given the grace of loving my enemies."

During his prison years, each day became a time of Sabbath worship, a light in his darkness and a source of courage flowing from the adoration of God and the graces of salvation flowing from the Mass.

Prayer

Jesus, Bread of life, Lord of the Sabbath, we praise you for the gift of the celebration of the Eucharist. We believe this sacrament contains your sacrificial love by which we are able to share in your death and resurrection. We also affirm in faith that in Communion we receive your Body and Blood. Give us the graces to appreciate the Mass as your gift by which we best fulfill the call to Sabbath worship. At the same time, help us realize the benefits of your other call to Sabbath rest by which we get in touch with creation, the Creator and our covenant relationship with you. AMEN.

The Lord of angels became man so that man could eat the bread of angels. (Saint Augustine, Sermon 13)

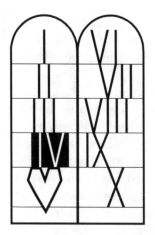

CHAPTER FOUR

Fourth Commandment

Family Values

Honor your father and your mother.... Children, obey
your parents (in the Lord), for this is right.

—DEUTERONOMY 5:16; EPHESIANS 6:1

It Takes a Neighborhood to Raise a Child

The fourth commandment opens the second table of
the Decalogue... [which deals with the love of neighbor)].... God has willed that, after him, we should
honor our parents to whom we owe life and who have
handed onto us the knowledge of God. (CCC, 2197)

Political speechwriter Peggy Noonan produced a family
values program for PBS. She interviewed three people,
all of whom said, "It takes a village to raise a child." The
image evoked nostalgic memories of storybook families in
quiet rural settings, or in yeasty ethnic neighborhoods from
the years before World War II, with two-parent families,
two sets of grandparents and lots of aunts, uncles, cousins
and neighbors.

The spiritual heart of these villages and neighborhoods
was the church or synagogue, with strong support from the
local school, be it parochial or public. Garrison Keillor
recovered that vision with gentle humor in his *Prairie Home*

Companion sketches with his signature closing line, "And now we leave Lake Wobegone, where all the women are strong and all the men are good looking and all the children are above average."

These idyllic scenes stir up memories of days when children were taught obedience and respect for parents, adults and public leaders, of times when the elderly were mostly cared for at home, of eras when fathers trained (and civilized) their sons—and mothers nurtured their daughters. Though village and neighborhood family life was not perfect, it reminds us of ideals. Such goals are sustained by the Fourth Commandment—and the commandments that follow—which outlines family and civic virtues designed by God for our happiness, fulfillment and peace.

How Do You Honor Family Values?

The *Catechism of the Catholic Church* presents us with these ways to support family values:

- Renew the ideal of the family in society (page 70).

- Review the duties of parents and children to each other (page 74).

- Support the Church's Family Bill of Rights (page 82).

- **RENEW THE IDEAL OF THE FAMILY IN SOCIETY.** (*CCC*, 2201-2213)

  A man and a woman united in marriage, together with their children, form a family.... The relationships within the family bring an affinity of feelings, affections and interests, arising from all the members' respect for one another.... Authority, stability, and a life of relationships within the family constitute the foundations for freedom, security and fraternity within society. (*CCC*, 2202, 2206, 2207)

The *Catechism's* home truths about the family confront the tragic breakdown of family life in America. While I want to concentrate on the strengthening of family life, I must first list some painful facts. The most troublesome fact of all in American society is the prevalence of divorce and its devastating effect on family life and children.

Nearly two out of every five kids in America do not live with their fathers. David Blankenhorn, in his provocative book *Fatherless America: Confronting Our Most Urgent Social Problem* (New York: HarperCollins, 1996), argues that fatherlessness is the most destructive trend of our generation.

Absent fathers are linked to most of our social nightmares, boys with guns and girls with babies. Forty-six percent of families with children headed by single mothers live below the poverty line, compared to eight percent of those with two parents. A large number of kids do not live with their biological parents. Millions of deadbeat dads have abandoned child support—to the tune of 36 billion dollars owed this year alone. Only one child in six sees his separated dad once a week, often in a superficial relationship.

Judith Wallerstein, emeritus researcher at the University of California at Berkeley, began a study of children of divorce back in 1970 and has tracked the trend ever since. She recalls reporting that 18 months after the breakup, "We didn't see a single child that was well adjusted. Divorce can increase an adult's happiness but it is devastating to a child. Divorce is not just an episode in a child's life, it's like a natural disaster that changes the whole trajectory of a child's life."

On the positive side, the culture itself is finally waking up to the need to save marriage and the family. Lawyers have joined the battle. Lynne Gold-Bikin, a divorce lawyer who chairs the family law division of the American Bar Association, has founded the Preserving Marriages Project. She says divorce lawyers have no vested interest in saving marriages, but they know the problem more than anyone else. Every day lawyers see kids being yanked back and forth. "I'm sick of people not recognizing what they are doing," she says.

She has organized 3,200 lawyers to go to high school classrooms to talk about family law and help students to learn how to have a stable marital relationship. Next she hopes to convince corporations to sponsor marriage preservation projects by showing them how much divorce causes immense productivity loss.

Michael McManus, pastor of the Fourth Presbyterian Church in Bethesda, Maryland, likes to quote Malachi 2:16: "For I hate divorce, says the LORD." He has written a book called *Marriage Savers* (Grand Rapids, Mich.: Zondervan Publishing Company, 1995), which encourages ministers to require lengthy relationship counseling before marriage and to train older couples to serve as mentors to younger ones. He says, "We're preventing bad marriages. If it is the Church's job to bond couples for life, it has to provide more help before and after."

Three-quarters of Americans marry in a church or a synagogue. Ministers, priests and rabbis have a golden opportunity to prepare couples as thoroughly as possible for marriage and to help them save their marriages after the ceremony.

The Catholic Church has long required premarital counseling, Cana Conferences and a premarital inventory— a hundred-question tool about everything from money to sex, children and compatibility. The Church also prohibits divorce and sponsors marital stability through Marriage Encounter weekends, The Couple-to-Couple League and marital counseling. Catholicism encourages prayer, regular church attendance and active participation in the sacraments and spiritual building blocks for strengthening family life. By and large this works. The state of Massachussetts, with a very large Catholic population, has the lowest divorce rate in the nation.

Other religious-sponsored efforts to renew married life

include *Retrouvaille* and Promise Keepers. *Retrouvaille* recruits couples who have weathered their own marital problems to run seminars for other couples in trouble. The participants have been through the stages of marriage— romance, casual irritation and disillusionment. At the final stage, many couples decide to bail out. They don't realize they could work their way back to stable and happy relationships. At *Retrouvaille*, couples hear success stories of how to forgive one another and get over it and how to deal with conflict. Then they are taught how to do this themselves.

Evangelicals are working on fathers to motivate them to live up to their marriage vows. Rallies are held in stadiums around the country to inspire fathers to be "Promise Keepers." These rallies are followed by small group meetings of dads who pray over and discuss ways to deepen their marital commitments.

The *Catechism* urges governments and other social groups to help families achieve stability and cohesiveness. "The family must be helped and defended by appropriate social measures. Where families cannot fulfill their responsibilities, other social bodies have the duty of helping them and of supporting the institution of the family" (CCC, 2209).

Among the suggestions given to lawmakers is the termination of no-fault divorce. Tax laws should be reexamined to make them marriage-friendly and pro-family. Harder to get at but essential is the change in society's expectation of marriage and family. Expectation affects performance. If the culture turns around and begins to expect couples to stay married and makes their children's needs a priority, then that is what will happen.

Judith Wallerstein's latest book is an effort to do just that. In *The Good Marriage: How and Why Love Lasts* (New York: Warner Books, 1996), she documents the traits shared by couples who stayed married for decades. "The American way and the work ethic have to bend to meet the needs of adults and the children if we are to take the divorce rate seriously," said Wallerstein to an interviewer after the book's publication. "The home is a haven. Children absolutely need a family," she added.

Life Application

1) From your experience of family life in these fast-paced times, what advice would you give for strengthening families? How can religion contribute to the happiness and fulfillment and stability of families? Among families you consider to be coping well, what do you see as the main elements that make this happen?

2) Why does divorce have a negative impact on family life? Do you think the next generation will work more on their marriages and divorce less frequently? If your answer is yes, what is the basis of your judgment? What could the movers and shakers of culture do to improve family life?

3) It has often been said that a strong family is the basis of a flourishing society. Why is this so? On the other hand, studies from history, especially the collapse of the Roman Empire, link family breakdown with the demise of a nation. Why is this so? How can we reverse trends in the United States that strike at the integrity of the family?

- **REVIEW THE DUTIES OF PARENTS AND CHILDREN TO EACH OTHER.** (*CCC*, 2214-2231)

Honor Your Father and Your Mother

Respect for parents...derives from *gratitude* toward those who, by the gift of life, their love and their work, have brought their children into the world and enabled them to grow in stature, wisdom and grace.... Filial respect is shown by true docility and *obedience*.... The fourth commandment reminds grown children of their *responsibilities toward their parents*. (CCC, 2215-2216, 2218)

The Catholic family is the domestic Church. Just as God is the author of the Church, so God is the author of the family. Divine love brings the family into existence and calls its members to communion with each other. The bond of love that begins with husband and wife should flow into the broader communion of the family, of parents and children, of brothers and sisters, of relatives and other members of the household.

God has given each member of the family the graces and powers to create family solidarity so that it becomes a school of humanity and laboratory of virtues. In practical terms, this means a prevailing sense of loving and caring for one another, especially the most needy: the children, the sick, the elderly. In such an environment, each will share joys, sorrows and talents.

Between parents and children, a unique opportunity for enlarging communion with each other can develop when each gives and receives. When children love, respect and obey their parents, they make a positive and essential contribution to the process of building a true, human and Christian family. In this way, children activate the considerable gifts of their parents and release their energies of love, education and experience on behalf of the children.

When parental instincts are wedded to Christian faith, the parents identify their calling as a ministry to the human and Christian welfare of their children. Such parents serve their children well when they call them to responsible freedom. This is in fact a gift from the child to the parent, who is offered the remarkable chance to impart the virtues, both human and divine, that will give the child the possibility of proper adulthood. In this way, parents and children treat and welcome one another with dignity as human persons and images of God.

A spirit of sacrificial love should mark the relations between spouses as well as those between parents and children. Every family faces the trials of selfishness, anger, tension, quarrels and competing demands. All concerned must be open to the healing oil of forgiveness, reconciliation, understanding, generosity of heart, hugs and kisses that restore the unity of the family. God calls all families to the joy of renewing themselves with peace and love, especially through the Sacraments of Reconciliation and the Eucharist that communicate the graces of the Holy Spirit, moving families to overcome every division and strive for complete communion between themselves.

No Christian family can survive without prayer. Family prayer provides the experience of faith growth, which puts soul into the more explicit faith events of religious education and sacramental celebration. Yes, children must learn their doctrine and acquire the virtue of religion through regular participation in the sacraments. But without the environment of family prayer, which is to faith what fresh air and sunshine are for human health, the seeds of doctrine and sacraments will not fall on sufficiently receptive ground.

Pope John Paul II links family prayer to celebrations: "Family prayer has for its very own object family life, which is seen as a call from God and lived as a response to that call. Joys and sorrows, births and birthdays, wedding anniversaries of the parents, departures, separations and homecomings, important and far-reaching decisions, the deaths of loved ones—all are marks of God's loving interventions in the family's history. They should be seen as teachable moments for thanksgiving and trusting surrender of the family to God's loving care" (*The Role of the Christian Family*, 59).

Care of the Elderly

There was a time when the Fourth Commandment was invoked primarily for encouraging young children to obey their parents and other adult authority figures. But its original intent touched on the loving care of aging parents by their adult children.

Some scholars believe that the commandment was phrased negatively in the beginning: "You shall not curse your father or your mother." The positive way it is now stated clearly implies that aging parents deserve loving support from their adult offspring. Refocusing on the scriptural intention of this commandment opens its rich spiritual and moral meaning and enables the Church at large to make pastoral support of the family, the "domestic Church," a major priority.

In biblical times, aging parents who could no longer work to support themselves depended entirely upon their children to take care of them. Tragically, many nomadic tribes of the time left their elderly or sick parents behind to die. The Fourth Commandment speaks against cruelty to parents in ancient nomadic cultures and in any culture today. Israel was not to resemble other nations. Neither should Christian families today adopt callous cultural attitudes toward elderly parents. Families must stick together and help each other.

In Mark 7:11-12, Jesus speaks against using religious laws to mistreat one's parents. He condemns the practice whereby a son could put his savings under *Korban*, which meant it now belonged to God (though in fact the son would still use the money for his own interests). If parents came for economic assistance, he could say, "Sorry, Mom and Dad, I can't help you. My cash belongs to God." In repudiating such behavior, Jesus echoes the teaching of Proverbs 28:24, "He who defrauds father or mother and calls it no sin, / is a partner of the brigand."

Scriptural teaching expected that children would honor their parents, without whom they would not exist at all:

> With your whole heart honor your father; / your mother's birthpangs forget not. Remember, of these parents you were born; / what can you give them for all they gave you? (Sirach 7:27-28)

It is perhaps no mistake that the commandment about relationship to parents comes first after the commandments that deal with our relationship to God. Biblical commentator B. Davie Napier writes that God is in effect saying, "Your life is my gift. I created you in the image of the divine. Your life breath is transmitted through your parents. In this special way, my life impinges upon your life. The life your parents bear and give to you is my life. To dishonor them is to dishonor me." Such dishonor, therefore, is a way of breaking our covenant with God.

Scripture reminds adult children to provide for their elderly and helpless parents with a generous heart: "Listen to your father who begot you,/and despise not your mother when she is old" (Proverbs 23:22). Rich rewards from the affectionate hand of God await those who look after their parents in their retirement years: "He who honors his father atones for sins;/he stores up riches who reveres his mother..../[A]nd when he prays he is heard" (Sirach 3:3-4, 5b. Sirach 3:1-16 is a commentary on the Fourth Commandment.).

At the same time, the scriptural word delivers a harsh judgment on those who mistreat their parents: "He who mistreats his father, or drives away his mother,/is a worthless and disgraceful son" (Proverbs 19:26). Such a person will be deprived of prosperity: "If one curses his father or mother,/his lamp will go out at the coming of darkness" (Proverbs 20:20). The biblical text rises to superheated scorn of those who abandon and betray their parents: "The eye that mocks a father,/or scorns an aged mother,/Will be plucked out by the ravens in the valley;/the young eagles will devour it" (Proverbs 30:17). In other words, the craven son or daughter will be denied burial; the body will be thrown into a field to be devoured by carrion birds. Strong words indeed for those who would betray the most binding of human relationships, that of parents and children!

The Elderly in America

Loyalty to the family bond in obedience to scriptural teaching is under great strain in modern America. It used to be that most people did not age. They died. In 1776, a newborn child could expect to reach thirty-five years of age. Today Americans can live well into their nineties. In 1950, people sixty-five or older made up just seven percent of the population. Now the number is twelve percent, and the fastest-growing age group is eighty-five and over.

While many of the elderly are living healthy and productive lives, there is also the haunting presence of the elderly poor, most of them widows and many of them black. Many of them are sick and getting sicker, as health care costs mushroom beyond their means. The government is torn between finding money for both child care and Medicare, for education and catastrophic health insurance. Advances in medical science cause doctors, moralists and lawmakers to wonder if they will have to ration health care between the young and the old.

Some people are talking about an age war between the hapless working young and the organized elderly. (The American Association of Retired Persons, at 28 million members, is bigger than most nations.) The elderly fight to preserve Medicare, Social Security and other programs that protect senior citizens from destitution.

But it is unwise to foster an intergenerational debate, an age war. Meeting the needs of young and old alike is a matter of social justice, not age. "I don't think this should ever be put in terms of equity, that there is a choice between the elderly and children," states Alan Pifer, coeditor of *Our Aging Society: Paradox and Promise* (New York: W.W. Norton & Company, 1986). "There are many other questions. The central issue is how to protect those in society who are most vulnerable, regardless of age."

Meanwhile, "sandwich" families suffer awesome strain as they try to raise their children and care for their parents on a squeezed household budget. The graying of America presents new and more difficult problems for the adult children of aging parents. Extended life spans and rising medical costs place severe stress on their growing families. The good news is that, according to Elaine Brodie of the Philadelphia Department of Human Services, "Today's adult children provide more care to more elderly parents over longer periods of time than ever before. The vast majority of services to the elderly are provided by the family and not the government."

The family remains the major source of support for the elderly, and there are no signs that families will abandon their senior members in the future. Moreover, not only do adult children help their parents, but many of the elderly also help their children with money for down payments on homes and college education for the grandchildren.

Society must indeed help care for the elderly with government-sponsored aid, while all agree that a family is a greater source of compassion than a federal agency. Beyond this, corporations are awakening to their responsibility for workers stressed by the demands of giving care. Some companies offer flextime, information fairs where employees meet social service experts, lunchtime support groups, seminars and handbooks on care of the elderly and partial repayment for parent-sitters on evenings and weekends. Further, the resources of the elderly are being tapped for the young: Local communities are matching up skilled retirees with young people who need training and guidance. A foster grandparent program is growing.

The elderly who have no adult children to care for them need considerate and thoughtful surrogate adult children to look in on them. *The Washington Post* reported on just such a person: a twenty-six-year-old sailor named Christopher Webster, who won a Navy public service award for his thoughtfulness. This young petty officer has a passionate commitment to donating time, effort and attention to people who need more than a Social Security check and a hot meal. He befriends people who have no one in their final years. "They deserve better than that," he says.

He tells about "Miss Rose," an eighty-two-year-old woman who liked the flowers he brought her, but hinted she would enjoy pizza and beer more. Isolated in a shabby apartment building, a wheelchair user without friends or family, she cried from sheer loneliness.

Occasionally Christopher cooked a meal for her while she talked about earlier, happier times. Her husband, who had died 40 years before, had helped build the Lincoln Memorial. Aging and alone, she needed nothing so much as company. Miss Rose died three months after Christopher met her. He intends to keep up his friendly visits to the aged—and hopes there is a support group for him in his old age.

An agency called the Little Brothers—Friends of the Elderly, with branches in the United States, Europe and Canada, serves people who have no one to help them. Clients over sixty-five (seventy in some locations) come mostly through referrals from social workers. Staff members visit the referred persons and then attempt to match them with volunteers. The services include regular and holiday visiting, help with shopping, moving and medical appointments, small group outings and vacation sessions.

Parishes have also proved an asset to the elderly by providing volunteer visitors, social events at the parish center, volunteer transport to doctors, dentists and shopping, prayer support groups and many other services.

Life Application

We now see that honoring father and mother operates at two levels: the relationship between young children and parents and the one between adult children and their elderly parents. We also note that duties and responsibilities go both ways—from children to parents and from parents to children. This gives us much to think about:

1) How do we nourish loving obedience in our children?

2) What is needed to improve care of our children?

3) How well do we nurture faith growth in our children?

4) Do we spend sufficient time with our families?

5) Are we involved in our children's education?

6) Do our children understand the role of respect for us?

7) How are we coping with the needs of our elderly parents?

8) Who can help us with strengthening our families?

9) How do we deal with suffering and death in our family life?

- **SUPPORT THE CHURCH'S FAMILY BILL OF RIGHTS.** (*CCC*, 2211, 2234-2246)

> The importance of the family for the life and well-being of society entails a particular responsibility for society to support and strengthen marriage and the family. Civil authority should consider it a grave duty "to acknowledge the true nature of marriage and the family, to protect and foster them, to safeguard public morality, and promote domestic prosperity." (*CCC*, 2210)
>
> Ideally, the family and society should support one another. In reality, this is not always the case. In some cases, governments enact laws that unjustly violate the essential rights of families (such as coercive abortions in China). There are cultures that fail to serve the family and violently attack family values. The failure of American law to supervise violent media entertainment is one instance. The forthcoming deregulation of TV in view of the imminent fiber optic "five hundred channels," only signals a worse, not a better, situation. In these cases, the family, which is the basic unit of society, becomes its victim.

The Church openly and strenuously defends the rights of the family in the face of these oppressive measures of state and culture. The Synod of Bishops at Rome in 1980 issued a Bill of Rights on behalf of families. Here are some of them:

> The right to exist and progress as a family, that is, the right of every human being, even if he or she is poor, to found a family and to have adequate means to support it.

> The right to exercise its responsibility regarding the transmission of life and to educate children.

> The right to believe in and profess one's faith and to propagate it.

> The right, especially of the poor and sick, to obtain physical, social, political and economic security.

> The right to protect minors by adequate institutions and legislation from harmful drugs, pornography, alcoholism, etc. (*The Role of the Christian Family*, 46; *CCC*, 2211)

The family existed before the state and does not receive its legitimacy from a government. Both natural law and revelation are the sources of the inalienable rights of the family listed above. As *Gaudium et Spes* has taught, the human person is the center and crown of creation. It is in Jesus Christ that the full dignity and potential of a person may be seen and understood (cf. *Gaudium et Spes*, 12, 22). The family is the best place to nourish and protect this vision. Governments and cultures ignore this to their peril, for the breakdown of the family beckons the very dissolution of those forces that oppress it.

The rich teaching of the *Catechism* on the family as seen through the lens of the Fourth Commandment deserves much more reflection than these few pages can contain. I urge my readers to study two synodal documents: *Familiaris Consortio (The Role of the Christian Family)* and *Christifidelis Laici (The Lay Members of Christ's Faithful People)* for the wise and temperate guidance they give on these crucial issues of family values.

Family Prayer

Family prayer nourishes the faith of both parents and children. The term *family prayer* often makes one think of everyone kneeling by the bed, hands folded and eyes lowered. But that sentimental picture is too limiting. For one thing, it associates prayer with nightly arguments about going to bed. The right time for prayer depends on each family's situation.

Little ones should be allowed to pray at their own pace. If they are not ready, they can play quietly while the older family members pray.

Music helps prayer along. Saint Augustine says that he who sings prays twice. Simple and lively songs are best.

Participation by lighting a candle, holding the Bible, sprinkling holy water, giving the blessing, peace hugs and so forth give the participants a sense of ownership of the prayer.

Honesty in praying to God is an attitude that reinforces religious teaching. Authentic prayer is love of God, self and others; therefore it should include concern for others. In Irish tradition the intercessions for others were called "trimmin's." Some families posted the "trimmin's" or prayer list (remembrances of birthdays and anniversaries, thank-you's for favors received, petitions for the sick and similar concerns), on the refrigerator.

Family prayer time should be short, surely no longer than 15 minutes and certainly no longer than 5 minutes for the very little ones. On a regular basis, a family might consider a reconciliation prayer: "I'm sorry I treated you that way." "I apologize for all the trouble I made for you." Perhaps this is truly where the hug works best as a prayer conclusion. Lastly, take time to answer the "why questions" about kneeling, making the sign of the cross, folded hands and so on. Sometimes parents even ask the questions to help children reflect on what's happening.

Regarding family prayer, John Paul II writes, "In prayer, Christian parents penetrate the depths of their children's hearts and leave an impression that future events in their lives will not efface" (*The Role of the Christian Family*, 60). In Christian prayer, parents express their priesthood and activate the baptismal priesthood of their children.

Paul VI appealed to parents to pray with their children:

> "Mothers, do you teach your children the Christian prayers? Do you prepare them, along with your pastor, for the sacraments of Confession, Communion and Confirmation? Fathers, do you pray with your children? Your example of honesty in thought and action, coupled with family prayer, is a lesson in life for your children, an act of worship of singular value. In this way you bring peace to your homes." (Quoted by John Paul II in *The Role of the Christian Family*, 60)

Educating children in the ways of faith includes sharing with them the history of salvation and above all the gospel of Christ. While children are thus educated in religious knowledge, it is essential that they also be trained in the practice of faith, hope and love. Parents will find a rich set of spiritual values in the Bible with which they can guide their children, both by word and example, for parental modeling of gospel values is a powerful method for leading children to know and practice moral principles.

Growing in Faith

1) How can we tell from Scripture that God is the author of families and remains vitally concerned about family values?

2) Why is human and Christian communion essential for the development of family values?

3) Why are sex, sadism and violence in films, popular

music, TV and other forms of popular entertainment injurious to the ideals of family life?

4) How can families, parishes and dioceses cooperate to implement the Synod of Bishops' (1980) declaration of the "Rights of Families"?

Growing in Knowledge

1) There are new movements within the culture and various religious groups to renew family life. What currents of renewal have you found helpful for your family growth?

2) What are some practical ways that parents and children can come to appreciate each other's gifts and so welcome one another as human persons and images of God?

3) What have you been able to do to make family prayer an essential part of your family life?

4) Why is it said that a faith environment in a family produces a receptive ground for a child's understanding of Catholic doctrine and sacramental practice?

Meditation

Certain images fix family values in our consciousness. When Norman Rockwell paints a Thanksgiving dinner, the turkey and the trimmings are framed by grandparents, parents and grandchildren with heads bowed in prayerful thanks. At such times, the family meal seems to say it all.

Poetry has long celebrated the values of the loving home:

So blest are they who have within their home
That touch of kinship—folks they call their own—
Flesh of their flesh: Ah, how they earnest strive
To ease the small tensions, keeping love alive,

If once they knew the desolate despair
That haunts the house with no one waiting there.
So blest are they who round a family board
May gather—May they humbly thank the Lord,
Not only for the food they common share,
But for the dear, loved faces circled there:
So oft, unless we face that board alone,
We treasure not its true, sweet sense of home.

—DONNA R. LYDSTON

Prayer

Jesus, Mary and Joseph, we are inspired by the family
witness you gave us from Nazareth. The simplicity, faith
and love you demonstrated are just what we are looking
for today. The prayer that filled your home is exactly
what we need now. The moral behavior that you show us
is a goal that we can realize with divine help. Jesus, give
us the grace of family values so that we may live out the
mystery of your salvation by which you free us from our
sins and flood us with divine graces. We praise you Lord,
now and forever. AMEN.

Parent: What did you learn in religion class today?
Child: We studied the top ten commandments.

87

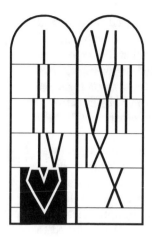

CHAPTER FIVE

Fifth Commandment

Playing God With Human Life

You shall not kill.—EXODUS 20:13

You have heard that it was said to your ancestors, 'You shall not kill; and whoever kills shall be liable to judgment.' But I say to you that every one who is angry with his brother shall be liable to judgment....

—MATTHEW 5:21–22

Does My Existence Make You Uncomfortable?

A few years ago, *U.S. News & World Report* published a cover story about euthanasia and Dr. Kevorkian's assisted suicide interventions. Among the many fine subsequent letters to the editor, the following deserve repeating here.

> A collective thank-you from hospices worldwide for your splendid cover story. It is indeed an outrage that we should want to kill the sufferer rather than relieve the suffering. We are a nation believing in choice and, until your story appeared, hospices' incredible ability to help terminally ill patients and their families was back page news.—*Barbara Borman*
>
> I was born with a disability. As a child I spent a lot

89

of time in severe pain. Today, I use a wheelchair, and lead an active and fulfilling life. To those who argue so vehemently for my "right" to end that life, I have one question: Are you truly concerned about my human dignity, or does my existence simply make you so uncomfortable that you would rather I disappear? To me this "right to die" sounds more like society's right to kill me.—*Douglas Lathrop*

As a blind, partially hearing wheelchair user, I was insulted when those were the physical characteristics used by Kevorkian's attorney to describe a life of absolutely no value in justification of his employer's "assistance" in helping one woman to die. That "patient" as well as those others who have turned to him, deserved adequate treatment and support, not death.—*Mary Jane Owen* (16 May 1994)

Do You Believe in the Gospel of Life?

The *Catechism of the Catholic Church* lays out for you the basis for the sacredness of human life:

- Respect human life (page 90).

- Reverence the dignity of persons (page 96).

- Safeguard peace (page 100).

• **RESPECT HUMAN LIFE.** (*CCC*, 2259-2283)

The car bomb that robbed 169 innocent adults and children of life in Oklahoma City has exploded much of the indifference our national conscience may have cherished about the sacredness of life. The Fifth Commandment is meant to protect human life and speaks against willful murder. Besides terrorism, this commandment also addresses incendiary issues such as abortion, euthanasia (deliberate killing of the aged or infirm), use of human embryos for medical research, war and capital punishment.

Pope John Paul's encyclical, *Evangelium Vitae* (*The*

Gospel of Life), splendidly complements the *Catechism of the Catholic Church's* teaching about life and death. The pope contrasts the world's "culture of death" to the Bible's "culture of life." From the story of Cain and Abel, through the prophets and psalms, the pope sees the Hebrew Bible testifying to the God-given gift of life. Killing the innocent denies the human dignity of people born in the image of God. Jesus taught and witnessed the very same message.

> *Human life is sacred* because from its beginning it involves the creative action of God and it remains forever in a special relationship with the Creator, who is its sole end. God alone is the Lord of life from its beginning to its end: no one can under any circumstances claim for himself the right directly to destroy a human being. (*CCC*, 2258)

Read the above words out loud, slowly. Then think of them in the cultural climate of the West where life is threatened at its beginning and end by abortion and euthanasia, precisely at the weakest moments in human life. Think also of those who argue that such terminations of life are "human rights" that should be protected by civil authority and law.

> The inalienable rights of the person must be recognized by civil society and the political authority.... Among such fundamental rights one should mention...every human being's right to life from the moment of conception until death.... As a consequence of the respect and protection which must be ensured for the unborn child from the moment of conception, the law must provide appropriate penal sanctions for every deliberate violation of the child's rights. (*CCC*, 2273, 2270)

While Pope John Paul II urges all Catholics to build the Gospel of Life into their families and parishes as a formal mission, he also warns that anyone—father, mother, family, friend, doctor, hospital administrator, politician or publicist—who promotes choice in abortion shares in the sin of destroying life.

The pope says that politicians cannot separate private conscience from public conduct. In countries where abortion and euthanasia are legal, politicians may support laws that restrict but do not outlaw these practices, such as legislating against partial birth abortion. These laws are inherently unjust, and they promote the freedom of the strong against the weak. "Society has the right to protect itself against the abuses which can occur in the name of conscience and under the pretext of freedom" (*Evangelium Vitae*, 71). The pope sees in these developments an "eclipse of conscience." Opponents should resist civil and political approval of abortion and euthanasia with nonviolent and conscientious objection (cf. *Evangelium Vitae*, 73).

For women who have had abortions, the pope notes the pressures, fears and personal circumstances that mitigate a woman's subjective responsibility for her acts. While procuring or performing an abortion incurs excommunication, the medicinal (not punitive) purpose of excommunication is conversion and reconciliation with Christ and the Church. Forgiveness and grace can beget a spiritual and moral renewal. He urges these women to redeem their experience by becoming leaders in defense of the unborn and other vulnerable people.

Don't Play God With Embryos

The arrival of in vitro fertilization (IVF) affords the medical and scientific community the opportunity to "play God" with the very sources of life itself. The artificial reproduction that yields the possibility of test-tube babies has introduced a new way of breaking both the Fifth and Sixth Commandments. By removing the seed from the man and the egg from the woman with the intention of forming a human embryo outside the womb, the couple and the technician bypass the conjugal act.

In terms of the Fifth Commandment, there are further

considerations. The IVF techniques have a high rate of failure regarding fertilization as well as in the development of the embryo, which is exposed to the risk of death, often quickly. "The number of embryos produced is often greater than that needed for implantation in the woman's womb. These so-called 'spare embryos' are then destroyed or used for research. Under the pretext of scientific or medical progress this reduces human life to the level of simple 'biological material' to be freely disposed of" (*Evangelium Vitae*, 14).

What then of prenatal diagnosis? *Prenatal diagnosis* is morally licit "if it respects the life and integrity of the embryo and the human fetus and is directed toward its safeguarding or healing as an individual....It is *gravely opposed to the moral law* when this is done with the thought of possibly inducing an abortion, depending upon the results: a diagnosis must not be the equivalent of a death sentence" (*CCC*, 2274).

Many couples want a baby and feel angry and demoralized by their loss. They may harbor resentment against each other, the Church and even God. Their feelings are understandable and must be addressed honestly, openly, sensitively. The Church stands with these couples, presenting them a full range of legitimate choices, including medical treatments that assist rather than replace the conjugal act, and the option of adoption.

Beyond IVF is the field of embryo research. A panel at the National Institute of Health has recommended federal funding of embryo research. NIH set these guidelines (please remember that the Catholic Church rejects all human embryo research).

Acceptable
— creating embryos solely for research purposes
— studies to improve successful pregnancies
— research on process of fertilization
— studies on embryonic stem cells

Not Acceptable
— cloning human embryos for transfer to the womb
— research on embryos after 14 days of development
— genetic diagnosis for sex selection
— cross-species fertilization
— attempted transfer of human embryos into non-human animals
— fertilization and gestation of eggs from aborted fetuses

Richard Doerflinger, associate director of the Secretariat for Pro Life Activities at the National Conference of Catholic Bishops, said the NIH proposals give no moral respect to human embryos at any stage. "They had already decided not to treat the embryo as human. Panelists on various occasions referred to these embryos as 'human tissue,' basically raw material for research, not having any human status at all. The so-called fourteen-day limit is merely a speed bump on the road to no limits. What is technologically possible is not necessarily morally permissible."

Euthanasia

Dr. Kevorkian won headlines with his assisted suicide activities. Jubilant activists predicted that right-to-die laws would spread like wildfire after Oregon passed Measure 16, legalizing doctor-assisted suicide, and other states introduced such bills. But Dr. Kevorkian finally received a jail sentence and state and federal courts have been ruling against the constitutional right to die.

The most important outcome to date is a decision written by John Noonan of the Ninth Circuit Court. He overruled the May 1994 decision of Judge Barbara Rothstein in *Compassion in Dying* v. *Washington State*. Judge Noonan cited four special reasons why this is a bad idea, paraphrased as follows:

1) We should not have physicians in the role of killers of

their patients. It would perversely affect their self-understanding and reduce their desire to look for cures for disease, if killing instead of curing were an option.

2) We should not subject the elderly and infirm to psychological pressures to consent to their own deaths.

3) We should protect the poor and minorities from exploitation. Pain is a significant factor in the desire for doctor-assisted suicide. The poor and minorities do not have much provision for alleviation of pain.

4) We should protect all the handicapped from societal indifference and antipathy and any bias against them.

Our opposition to euthanasia does not mean that extraordinary efforts are needed to keep people alive.

> Discontinuing medical procedures that are burdensome, dangerous, extraordinary, or disproportionate to the expected outcome can be legitimate. Here one does not will to cause death; one's inability to impede it is merely accepted. (*CCC*, 2278)

Nonetheless, dying patients deserve our care. Even if death is thought imminent, the ordinary care owed to a sick person cannot be legitimately interrupted. The use of painkillers to alleviate the sufferings of the dying, even at the risk of shortening their days, can be morally in conformity with human dignity, if death is not willed either as an end or a means but only foreseen and tolerated as inevitable.

These general principles must guide us in the many agonizing decisions related to death and dying. Pastoral problems and conscience dilemmas will continue to spread as technology advances and new questions arise. As you search for practical answers, I would recommend reading Archbishop Daniel Pilarczyk's *Twelve Tough Issues* (Cincinnati: St. Anthony Messenger Press, 1988).

On a further positive note, we must celebrate the God of life in our hearts and the gift of eternal life from which all other life proceeds. We are called to care for everyone, especially those who are poorest, most alone, most in need. It is our calling to make the Gospel of Life penetrate the heart of every man and woman and every part of society by proclamation, catechesis, preaching, dialogue and education. The issue of life and its defense is the duty not only of Christians but of every person on earth.

Life Application

1) What are means that you have used to deepen your appreciation of the mystery and wonder of human life? How does the life of Jesus help you understand the importance of each and every human life?

2) Why is it important to defend life at every stage from conception to death? Why is faith so critical in standing up for human life? How can you guide infertile married couples to seek legitimate solutions to their painful dilemma? What are you doing to make the Gospel of Life a reality in your personal life, your family, your parish and community?

3) What are the positive moral means available for treating dying people with love, compassion, care and affection? What efforts are you making to counter the spread of abortion and euthanasia and embryo research?

• **REVERENCE THE DIGNITY OF PERSONS.** (*CCC*, 2284-2301)

The Smile Button

> The shortest distance between two people is a smile. In December 1963, the State Mutual Life Assurance Company was having a moral problem because of a merger. They asked an artist, Harvey Ball, to draw a smile to be used as a button to cheer up the people in the office. He should just paint a smile, nothing else, no eyes, no nose.

"I had a choice," Ball said, "I could have used a compass and made it as neat as possible, but I drew it freehand to give it some character." He liked his slightly crooked smile—but there was a problem. "A smile upside down is a frown." So he added two eyes and colored it yellow. The insurance company initially made a hundred buttons. Ball made forty-five dollars for the job. Everyone was happy.

But a few years later, two novelty manufacturers married the words, "Have a nice day," to the smiley face, and the rest is history. An estimated fifty million buttons have been made since 1971. Harvey Ball never trademarked the smiley face, so he never made any more money on the button.

"It doesn't bother me that I never made a lot of money on it. Money isn't everything. You can only drive one car at a time; you can only eat one steak at a time."

Recently, Harvey celebrated his seventy-fifth birthday. He has learned that happiness is not a birthday cake, nor making millions on a cultural icon. "You have to put it into perspective. My life changed on Saturday, April 21, 1945 at 4 p.m., on the island of Okinawa. Bingo! A Japanese mortar shell exploded right in front of me. It killed my two buddies to the left, it killed the guy in front of me, and wounded the guy to my right. I was unhurt. That changes your attitude. I was happy to be alive. I think doing the best you can and living responsibly will make you happy." (Adapted from "Are We Happy Yet?" by Stan Grossfield, *Boston Globe Sunday Magazine* [19 January 1997], 14-15, 66)

Harvey Ball created a little icon that celebrates human dignity. Our modern world is full of so much complexity, so many new issues brought about by the revolution in technology that the reality and beauty of human beings tends to get lost.

The ultimate source of our dignity is that we are images of God. What does this mean? It means that we have minds that can know the truth, which is the food of the intellect. We have desires for love, which is the nourishment of the heart.

We have boundless imaginations, which break the bonds of routine and unlock the creativity of scientists, artists, philosophers and anyone who wants to explore the riotous possibilities of our creation. We have passions and emotions that are at the service of our minds and hearts. Father Bernard Lonergan writes that we are unrestricted drives to know and be known, to love and be loved.

Another quality related to being God's images is the Lord's gift of freedom to us. This works best when it is tied to responsibility, a response to God's will for our well-being. While freedom is usually spoken of in terms of the ability to choose either good or evil, it should be noted that freedom is weakened when we pick the bad and expanded when we select the good.

We become more free with each act that moves to goodness. We are less free when we choose evil. Our society prizes "choice." This is fine so long as the choice is for love, peace, justice, goodness, prudence, courage and all virtues that correspond to God's plan for our salvation. Unfortunately, many in our culture think of the very act of choice as sufficient without reference to the object of the decision. This purely subjective approach to freedom and choice divorces it from an objective moral order.

Jesus shows us the proper approach to freedom and choice. He always relates it to the will of the Father. "Not everyone who says to me, 'Lord, Lord,' will enter the kingdom of heaven, but only the one who does the will of my Father in heaven" (Matthew 7:21). "My Father, if it is not possible that this cup pass without my drinking it, your will be done" (Matthew 26:42). And we all know the beginning of the Our Father that calls us to pray, "Thy will be done."

The Church values human freedom just as much as the culture and sees that it is intrinsic to respect for human dignity but also forges a solid bond between freedom and

God's will and the choice for good alone. We will exult in freedom the more we pick the good.

The slaughters of the twentieth century—the holocaust and other genocides—remind us of malevolent people who misused human freedom to enslave and butcher millions of humans. The holy value of a human being was ignored and the result was a rampant immorality that treated persons as things to be beaten, burned, humiliated and hurt.

The insistent message of the Fifth Commandment is that murdering people would not happen if we truly saw them as images of God to be revered, honored and protected from all deliberate harm.

The *Catechism* explores several interesting applications of this reverence for the person. Under the title of honoring the human soul, the *Catechism* teaches that we should avoid scandalizing people. Those who currently trade in shocking people should listen to this. Jesus spoke against those who scandalize others and try to lead them into sin when he said, "Whoever causes one of these little ones who believe in me to sin, it would be better for him to have a great millstone hung around his neck and to be drowned in the depth of the sea" (Matthew 18:6).

It is also fascinating to find that the *Catechism* invites us to take good care of our health. It teaches us that life and health are precious gifts entrusted to us by God. We should take care of ourselves and look after the needs of others and the common good.

> Concern for the health of its citizens requires that society help in the attainment of living-conditions that allow them to grow and reach maturity: food and clothing, housing, health care, basic education, employment, and social assistance. (*CCC*, 2288)

Allied to this concern for health is the *Catechism's* cautions about the cult of the body, drug addiction and abuse of food, alcohol, tobacco and medicine. Also considered here is kidnapping and hostage taking, terrorism and torture, all of which contravene the moral law.

In all these cases, the Church is raising our awareness of the basic respect due the human being as an image of God and someone destined to eternal glory and happiness.

Reflection

1) How have you experienced yourself growing in freedom?

2) When have you been treated as less than human?

3) What changes does our culture need to advance human dignity?

4) Name examples of people who illustrate genuine humanity.

5) How does one hit the balance between being healthy and the cult of the body?

• **SAFEGUARD PEACE.** (*CCC*, 2302-2317)

Blessed are the peacemakers,/for they will be called children of God. (Matthew 5:9)

Jesus made the search for peace one of his eight beatitudes. The Fifth Commandment contains the challenge of peace as well as the opposition to killing. In our first two points, we explored the teaching of the Fifth Commandment regarding abortion, euthanasia and other medical-moral issues. Here we listen to its message about war and peace—and the death penalty.

Pope John XXIII published his most powerful and inspiring encyclical, *Pacem in Terris* (*Peace on Earth*), on Holy Thursday, April 11, 1963. The world had just pulled back from the brink of nuclear war in the Cuban Missile Crisis. So appealing was his message that it was printed in full by *The New York Times*. *Time* magazine declared him Man of the Year because of his work for peace.

His blueprint for peace centered on the need to respect the dignity of the human person. Practically, this means defending the rights of all peoples. Pope John stated that these rights included what a person needs for basic survival, religious and political freedom, education in culture and technology, the ability to raise a family, work that is both satisfying and properly remunerative, ownership of property, freedom to join associations and unions, freedom to emigrate and participate actively in the political process.

The state should protect and advance these rights. Without the justice supported by these rights, there can be no peace. Pope John quoted Saint Augustine on this point, "Take away justice, and what are kingdoms but mighty bands of robbers" (*Pacem in Terris*, 92).

By using "rights language" the pope was able to appeal to all people of goodwill. But this did not stop him from deploying the full force of the Christian message. Pope John spoke of peace as a free gift, a grace from Christ, the prince of peace (*Pacem*, 167). Peace is not attainable by human efforts alone, essential as they are.

This stirring call to peace caught the world's imagination, partly because it came from someone who had no power in the conventional sense. Its authority arose from the cogency of what was said and the hope it inspired. It remains the only encyclical that has been set to music—by the French composer Darius Milhaud.

At our everyday level, we can promote peace in a variety of ways. Among these, I suggest first that we honor and revere the sacredness of each person we meet as an image of God. Secondly, I would take Pope John's list of rights and use them as a daily reminder of what we need to do for our neighbor, our community and our country.

This will involve banishing our angers, hatreds and biases toward others. It means making positive efforts to improve the social conditions of those who need our help. It means active participation in the political process so that the government is responsive to people's basic rights.

The protection of human rights always includes the call to civic and religious duties. Every right has a corresponding duty. If I have a right to a decent education, I also have a duty to be a responsible learner and to help others have the same opportunities I have. The kids of the 1960s used to sing, "Give peace a chance." This will happen when we are vigilant about justice, love and mercy for every human being.

The old saying that "all's fair in love and war" is not Christian teaching. Just because a war has started does not mean the moral law has stopped. Genocide is unacceptable. The indiscriminate destruction of whole cities and their inhabitants is wrong. Wounded soldiers and prisoners of war deserve proper and humane treatment.

The development of modern scientific weapons— nuclear, biological and chemical—has vastly increased the destructive potential of today's warfare. This new situation makes one wonder how the Church's "just war" teaching can be applied today. While admitting the legitimate right of self-defense (2308), the *Catechism* outlines the principles of just war doctrine as follows:

> The strict conditions for legitimate defense by military force require rigorous consideration. The gravity of such a decision makes it subject to rigorous conditions of moral legitimacy. At one and the same time:
>
> — the damage inflicted by the aggressor on the nation or community of nations must be lasting, grave and certain;
>
> — all other means of putting an end to it must have been shown to be impractical or ineffective;
>
> — there must be serious prospects of success;
>
> — the use of arms must not produce evils and disorders graver than the evil to be eliminated. The power of modern means of destruction weighs very heavily in evaluating this condition. (*CCC*, 2309)

The just war doctrine has been invoked several times in recent history. During the Vietnam War, it provided the criteria whereby American citizens, without being pacifist, rejected the war. This included several thousand "selective conscientious objectors." In 1983, the Roman Catholic bishops of the United States formally rejected nuclear war:

> Under no circumstances may nuclear weapons or other instruments of mass slaughter be used for the purpose of destroying population centers or other predominantly civilian targets. We do not perceive any situation in which the deliberate initiation of nuclear warfare on however a restricted scale can be morally justified....(*The Challenge of Peace: God's Promise and Our Response,* 147, 150, 159)

We should be less worried about justifying a given war and more concerned to stop war altogether. John Kennedy said, "Mankind must put an end to war, or war will put an end to mankind."

We should do all we can to stop the "logic" of retaliation and revenge. It is better to make room for dialogue and patient waiting, which is more effective than the hasty deadlines of war. On Calvary, Jesus mounted the "nonviolent" cross and spoke of forgiveness of enemies and the abolition of revenge.

Ultimately, peace is a gift from God. Humanly speaking, we must do all we can to achieve it. Divinely speaking, we must never stop imploring God with fervent prayer for this most precious gift of peace.

Capital Punishment

Without a doubt, convicted criminals should be punished and society must be protected from those who commit serious crimes. This can be accomplished by means other than the death penalty. It remains unprovable that it deters murderers. Victims' families frequently admit that the retribution does not give them the satisfaction they thought it would.

The Oklahoma City bombing makes our decision about what to do with violent criminals more difficult. The outrage and anger generated by this crime against humanity made the call for the death penalty for the guilty parties understandable. Indeed, Timothy McVeigh has been convicted of this crime and is scheduled for execution in May 2001. But this only fires up the antilife mind-set that has been created by the culture of death witnessed by abortions, euthanasia and the prevailing violent crime rate. We will not become more civilized by becoming more barbaric.

Pope John Paul II addresses the matter in his encyclical *Evangelium Vitae (The Gospel of Life)*. "The nature and extent of the punishment must be carefully evaluated and decided upon and ought not to go to the extreme of executing the offender except in cases of absolute necessity: in other words, when it would not be possible to defend society. Today, however, as a result of steady improvements in the organization of the penal system, such cases are very rare, if not practically non-existent" (56).

It is clear from this passage that the pope has interpreted the *Catechism's* teaching about the permissibility of the death penalty in a very restrictive sense. In his view, cases of extreme gravity mentioned by the *Catechism* are now "very rare, if not practically non-existent." His teaching has been incorporated into the modifications of the *Catechism*. (See paragraph 2267.)

This matter is best seen not through a legal argument about the death penalty nor against the background of danger and revenge, but in the light of the need for building a culture of life.

The life that we possess as human beings and that we have received from God is very different from the life of every other creature. This truth is obscured in our day, which makes us think of ourselves as merely advanced animals. Genesis tells us that humankind is the culmination of

God's labors. It clearly teaches the primacy of human life over the rest of creation. Human life is a divine breath that is breathed into us so that we may live.

The Gospel of Life is about eternal life, the life offered us through Jesus. Our lives as children of God become the "place" where God manifests himself. Our lives do not belong to us but to God our Creator and Father. The highest expression of respect for ourselves and others is the commandment to love one another as we love ourselves (see Leviticus 19:18).

It is through the words, actions and person of Jesus that we understand the complete truth about the value of human life. All the death issues we have discussed can only be solved by contemplating the life issues centered in Jesus Christ, who is our "resurrection and life" (John 11:25-26).

Growing in Faith

1) Which wars do you think were "just wars"? Why do you think so?

2) What are three ways you could reduce conflict in your family, your community, your country?

3) Why does Pope John XXIII argue that justice is the best way to assure peace in the world?

4) How could people be persuaded to see Pope John Paul II's point about the death penalty?

Growing in Knowledge

1) What stories could you tell that demonstrate we are living in a "culture of death"?

2) What practical methods have you undertaken to promote a "culture of life"?

3) What passages from the Bible convince you of the value of human life?

4) How do you help your children appreciate the precious value of human life?

Meditation

> If I can stop one heart from breaking,
> I shall not live in vain;
> If I can ease one life the aching,
> Or cool one pain…
> I shall not live in vain.

—EMILY DICKINSON, "LIFE"*

Prayer

Life-giving Father, how often we have heard we should choose life and celebrate it. Yet, every day we hear about murders, abortions, wars, death penalties and doctor-assisted suicides. We see the growth of the culture of death. Dear God, help us to rebuild a culture of life. Show us how to reach out to those who would destroy life, either at its inception or at its conclusion—or anywhere in between. May our prayers for life be constant and our efforts on behalf of life be persistent. Thank you for the gift of life. May we show our gratitude by defending it. AMEN.

No one can arbitrarily choose to live or die. The absolute master of such a decision is the Creator alone, in whom "We live and move and have our being." (Acts 17:28) (John Paul II, *Evangelium Vitae*)

---

* From *The Poems of Emily Dickinson*, Thomas H. Johnson, ed. (Cambridge, Mass.: The Belknap Press of Harvard University Press, 1979).

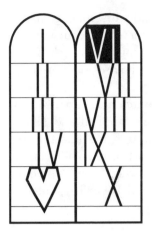

Sixth Commandment

God's Plan for Marriage and Sex

You shall not commit adultery.—EXODUS 20:14

You have heard that it was said, "You shall not commit adultery." But I say to you that everyone who looks at a woman with lust has already committed adultery with her in his heart.—MATTHEW 5:27-28

A Scene From a Marriage

Every day Eunice helps Henry up the stairs in front of their house atop a steep hill. He still does the driving around for them, but they are getting up in years. On warm evenings, they sit on their porch where they can watch neighbors mow lawns or tend children. Henry waits on Eunice, serving cold lemonade.

"We didn't think of getting old when we moved into this house with all its stairs thirty-eight years ago," Eunice says. But they remain there, being together, with the little things. Somehow just being in each other's presence makes all of life's challenges seem less important. Eunice and Henry, after a lifetime together, love each other.

What is Eunice and Henry's secret to happiness? They've learned and accepted that, over time, the little things add up to make a marriage. At the wedding, lofty promises are made before family and worshiping community. Newlyweds make plans in decades. But outside the exciting periods of transition—moving, having children, new jobs or whatever surprises life holds—most married life happens in the everyday.

It is in the everyday that the Church holds up the ideal of marriage, an ideal with roots in the Sixth and Ninth Commandments. The Church, through the tradition of marriage, holds up the path that most people will achieve holiness. In this chapter we will see how the Sixth Commandment contributes to this goal. We will explore the Ninth Commandment in Chapter Nine.

Do You Want to Live God's Plan for Sex and Marriage?

The *Catechism* outlines the faith ideals that will make this possible for you.

- Listen to the call for marital fidelity (page 108).

- Understand the unitive and procreative goals of marriage (page 111).

- Cultivate chastity (page 117).

• LISTEN TO THE CALL FOR MARITAL FIDELITY. (CCC, 2360-2391)

In Thornton Wilder's *The Skin of Our Teeth*,* Mrs. Antrobus says to her husband, "I didn't marry you because you were perfect, George. I didn't even marry you because I loved you. I married you because you gave me a promise. (She takes off her ring and looks at it.) That promise made up for your faults. And the promise I gave you made up for mine. Two imperfect people got married and it was the promise that made the difference."

The primary emphasis of the Sixth Commandment is

---

* From *3 Plays*. New York: Harperperennial Library, 1998.

not adultery so much as fidelity to the promises husbands and wives make to each other. That fidelity reflects what the Bible calls covenant. In the Hebrew covenant, marriage was meant to be an earthly mirror of the "wedding" between God and Israel.

God is the faithful spouse who loves Israel with irresistible affection. In the Christian covenant, marriage is meant to give us a visible reflection of Christ's "marriage" to his Church. Jesus is the faithful spouse who loves the Church so much he was willing to die for her.

Fidelity to the marital promise removes the imagined boundaries of love. More mutual pleasure results from inventive strategies to improve a marital relationship than from the soul-destroying secrecies of extramarital liaisons. Shakespeare spoke of the delights of fidelity in terms of unshakable love:

...Love is not love
Which alters when it alteration finds...
O, no! it is an ever-fixèd mark
That looks on tempests, and is never shaken;
It is the star to every wandering bark....(Sonnet 116)

A blessed assurance flows from fidelity, providing everyday comfortable security to husband and wife. Their response to each other's irrepressible desire for self-worth and dignity is the tenderest gift of one spouse to another.

The happiness that comes to a faithful couple often dazes them. The better they are at fidelity, the more they think themselves very lucky indeed. Each day they awake, they count themselves blessed to see the love in each other's eyes and confirm it with the embrace that brings their hearts together. The passing years make their love seem younger than when it first began.

Couples whose experience reveals the creative results of fidelity will be far more able to treat their children with an organic love rather than as a functional duty.

Young husbands should say to their wives: I have taken you in my arms and I love you, and I prefer you to my life itself. For the present life is nothing, and my most ardent dream is to spend it with you in such a way that we may be assured of not being separated in the life reserved for us.... I place your love above all things, and nothing would be more bitter or painful to me than to be of a different mind from you. (Saint John Chrysostom, Homily on Ephesians, 20,8)

Adultery and divorce break the promises of fidelity. Some biblical scholars note that the Hebrew word for adultery is similar to the word for idolatry. Since pagan temples in biblical times often employed prostitutes, those environments of idolatry were also havens for adultery. To engage in illicit sexual liaisons under the sign of a false god was also to enter into a false relationship with another person. Covenant acts take place in the sight of a living and true God. Unfaithful acts occur under the sign of delusion.

Fidelity in marriage means much more than abstaining from adultery. All religious ideals are positive, not negative. Husband and wife are pledges of eternal love. Their union in the flesh has a grace which prepares them for union with God. The passing of time wears out bodies, but nothing can make a soul vanish or diminish its eternal value. Nothing on earth is stronger than the fidelity of hearts fortified by the Sacrament of Marriage. They become like the unshakable columns of the Roman Forum against whom the ravages of time are powerless. Pleasure happens for a moment. Fidelity is an engagement for the future. (Archbishop Fulton J. Sheen, *Three to Get Married* [New York: Scepter Publications, 1996])

The Irish ring, the *claddagh*, symbolizes the basic picture of fidelity and how to maintain it. It shows hands folded in prayer around a heart of love, beneath a crown of fidelity.

Enduring prayer and everlasting love are the secrets of marital fidelity, which is itself the true secret of happiness.

Reflection

1) Think of stories about couples you know who witness marital fidelity. What is there about them that has made this possible? What could you learn from them? How have they dealt with the typical challenges married people normally face?

2) What have you done to make fidelity work for you in your marriage? What would you do to increase faithfulness between you and your spouse? How has faith and prayer been a source of strength for you in being faithful to your marriage vows?

3) Why is marital fidelity so important for the stability of children? Seen another way, what have you noticed about the children of divorce? What could the culture do to strengthen marriages?

• UNDERSTAND THE UNITIVE AND PROCREATIVE GOALS OF MARRIAGE. (CCC, 1638-1658)

Love Story

Some years ago in London a host of British VIPs, including Prime Minister Sir Winston Churchill and his wife, Lady Clementine, attended a banquet. It was a tradition at this particular banquet to play a little game before the main address by the guest speaker. The game that night was, "If you couldn't be who you are, who would you like to be?"

The honored guests answered the question in their own ways, but all waited with immense curiosity for Churchill's answer. Who else would he want to be? As the last speaker, he arose and said, "If I can't be who I am I would most like to be...," seventy-eight-year-old Winston turned to his wife and took her hand, "Lady Churchill's second husband."

Kept promises produce the kind of union sensed by the author of a *New Yorker* article: "Their enjoyment of each other was arresting—sharp as pepper, golden. I have seen other happy old couples, but this picture of the Joneses, renewed many times, came to represent to me the essence of human exchange. It showed me something indescribably moving and precious, which comes to fruition only after a lifelong marriage. It has struck me as one of the greatest possibilities life has to offer."

Unitive Love

The bond between husband and wife is both conjugal and procreative. Conjugal, mutual love is the unitive aspect of marriage. The *procreative* aspect of marriage concerns the conception, birth and education of children. The bond between the unitive and procreative may not be broken.

The unitive aspect of marriage involves the full personal unity of the spouses, a love that encompasses the minds, hearts, emotions, bodies, souls and aspirations of husband and wife. Their union in the flesh should lead to forming one heart and soul between them. They are called to grow continually so that they are no longer two but one flesh. Their mutual self-giving is confirmed, purified and completed by Jesus Christ in the Sacrament of Matrimony.

There are times when people think that a permanent love of spouses for each other seems difficult, even impossible. Then they need to remember that their love for one another should be rooted in the Good News that God loves them with an irrevocable love. Married couples can share in this marvelous divine love that supports and sustains them.

The consent that bride and groom give to each other is sealed by God himself in the sacrament. Real married love is united with divine love and shares in its beauty and permanence. God's love is reflected in the divine law that finds expression in the Sixth and Ninth Commandments. Biblically, this becomes concrete in God's covenant with Israel and Christ's covenant with the Church.

Love, covenant and law are three parts of the same reality. The law is an expression of divine affection that is never quenched and remains as both a model for marriage as well as a radical source of dynamic love available to the spouses.

The Holy Trinity is a loving community of persons. When God created man and woman in the divine image, he planted in them the call to love and gave them the capacity for intimate union.

Sexual intimacy expresses the unitive love of husband and wife. God, the author of marriage, created male and female. Sexual identity includes physical, moral and spiritual differences as well as complementarity. Men and women are different but meant to complement each other.

The man and woman possess equal dignity, for both were created in the image and likeness of God. Their sexual union is meant to be infused with love that grows deeper with the years and draws its power from the source of love who is God.

In the film *Indecent Proposal,* a rich bachelor offers a married woman a million dollars if she will spend one night with him. She persuades her husband that the bargain is worth it. "Well it's only my body, not my mind or emotions." With her husband's approval, she accepts the proposal. The rest of the story shows how the adultery nearly wrecks the marriage.

The *Catechism* could have saved them the trouble because it would tell them sex affects the whole person, not just the body. "*Sexuality* affects all aspects of the human person in the unity of his body and soul. It especially concerns affectivity, the capacity to love and procreate, and in a more general way the aptitude for forming bonds of communion with others" (*CCC,* 2332).

Jesus referred to the Genesis creation narratives in his teaching about marriage. When confronted with the practice of divorce in his time, he cited the doctrine of creation and applied it to the indissolubility of marriage. "They [husband and wife] are no longer two, but one flesh [cf. Genesis 2:24]. What God has joined together, no human

113

being must separate" (Matthew 19:6). In his Sermon on the Mount he taught that adultery is wrong and that lust is just as evil. "Everyone who looks at a woman with lust has already committed adultery with her in his heart" (Matthew 5:28).

The unitive love of the spouses is essentially related to the other aspect of the marital bond, namely, the procreative good of marriage.

Procreation

God calls the married couple to be open to having children. In this goal, they share in the creative power and father-hood of God. In giving birth to children and educating and forming them, married couples cooperate with the love of God as creator. Marital love of its nature is fruitful.

The destiny of marriage as a communion of love is to beget someone outside itself. The marriage act is meant to overflow into new life. Since God is present in all genuine acts of marital love, this love is not limited to the spouses. It goes into the immortal life of another person. God com-municates his power of creativity to the couple.

Many couples believe their love will last because their love is strong. But their love is more likely to mature because it is self-renewing. In having a child the couple lives out the paschal mystery. Husband and wife, in a sense, die to their present situation and rise again in the birth of their baby. The child is like a resurrection, bringing new and beautiful life that renews the marriage.

Children play a spiritual role in a family. They repre-sent the victory of love over the possibilities of marital ego-tism. Children inspire self-sacrifice in the parents. The parents learn that the mysterious reward of love is to spend itself on others. The child moves the parents away from a love in which they tend to possess one another to a self-for-getting love that is richer than the love they have known.

Children also inspire growth of a humble attitude

toward life. They make the adults feel little. They disarm their parents. A child invites us to be simple, to rediscover origins, even the origin of life itself—God. They are unconscious teachers of the fundamentals of the origin and destiny of life. The procreative good of marriage is a gift of God.

> A child does not come from outside as some thing to be added onto the mutual love of the spouses, but springs from the very heart of that mutual giving, as its fruit and fulfillment. So the Church, which is "on the side of life," teaches "that...each and every marriage act remain ordered to the procreation of human life." (*CCC*, 2366; *Humanae Vitae*, 11)

This passage from the *Catechism* flows from Church teaching that God established an inseparable bond between the unitive and procreative elements in a marriage. They may not be broken apart because they are inherent to the marriage act. This is why the Church considers artificial contraception and in vitro fertilization to be contrary to God's will for marriage.

Contraception is love without babies. In vitro fertilization is babies without love. Love and babies must go together. Every marital act must be one of love and open to the transmission of life.

Contemporary methods of Natural Family Planning (NFP) are making it possible for couples to space the births of their children while remaining faithful to the Church's teaching about the inseparable link between unitive and procreative aspects of marriage. For further study of this positive approach read "After Rhythm: The Development of NFP," *Ethics and Medics* [April 1995]. Also consult *Humanae Vitae: Making Happier Healthier Families*, audiocassettes by Dr. Janet Smith (West Covina, Calif.: St. Joseph Communications [phone: 626-331-3549]).

Pope Paul VI taught that a contraceptive mentality is a sterile vision of marriage, sex and family. Condoms and pills are wrong because they break the bond of love and procreation.

The *Catechism* lists the following acts as offenses against the dignity of marriage: adultery, divorce, incest, sexual abuse of children by adults, polygamy and living together without benefit of marriage.

Cohabitation undermines the dignity of marriage in several ways. It may involve the rejection of marriage as such or reflect the inability to make long-term commitments. It speaks of a "free union," but what can "union" mean when the partners make no real and lasting commitment to one another? Beneath the surface lingers the lack of trust. This situation dismisses the dignity of marriage, destroys the very idea of family and weakens the fidelity that is the true basis of a love relationship. "Carnal union is morally legitimate only when a definitive community of life between a man and a woman has been established" (*CCC*, 2391).

The spiritual dimension of marriage is essential. The more that married couples are in touch with God and his plan for marriage, the more they find in each other and their children the beauty and happiness that surpass everyday disappointments. Love songs never weary of celebrating lasting love. These popular melodies and lyrics are right. They echo the yearning for immortality that belongs to every heart.

God is permanent love. Couples who unite themselves to this dynamic current of love receive the gift of mutual affection. They are caught up in the source of the dream that brought them together in the first place. Christian marriage begins with a sacrament in which Christ joins them together in grace and agrees to walk with the couple until they are called to eternity. Marital growth is meant to be bound to the graces that the sacrament always makes available. The Sixth Commandment should always be studied together with the Sacrament of Matrimony. The graces of the sacrament support loving obedience to the commandment and make the burden light and the yoke sweet.

Growing in Faith

1) Why is the inseparable bond between the unitive and procreative aspects of marriage so central to our understanding of the Church's teachings on marriage and sex?

2) What are three powerful means at our disposal that can help teenagers and young adults prepare themselves for Christian marriage?

3) What stories of saints and heroes have inspired you to commit yourselves to lifelong self-mastery?

4) What can we do to transform our present secular culture into a world that supports God's plan for marriage and sex?

Growing in Knowledge

1) How does the secular culture's view of sex and marriage differ from that of Jesus and the Church?

2) How does Christian marriage reflect both the Hebrew and Christian covenants?

3) Why do we say that the Sixth Commandment's primary concern is fidelity rather than adultery?

4) What lessons do we learn from Genesis 1-3 about marriage?

• CULTIVATE CHASTITY. (CCC, 2337-2359)

The Book of Tobit tells the story of Sarah, whose first seven husbands all died on their wedding nights. The deaths were attributed to an evil demon. The angel Raphael accompanied young Tobiah to Sarah's house to become her eighth husband. Raphael instructed Tobiah to take fish liver and heart and mingle them with incense in the wedding chamber to drive away the demon. And the demon did flee.

When Tobiah and Sarah were alone, Tobiah said, "My love, get up. Let us pray and beg our Lord to have mercy on us and to grant us deliverance" (Tobit 8:4). In his prayer, Tobiah said, "Now, Lord, you know that I take this wife of mine,/ not because of lust,/ but for a noble purpose..." (8:7).

It is inferred from this part of the story that Sarah's previous husbands had approached the marital bed with lust and not with the intention of following God's full plan for marriage, which embraces both love and fruitfulness. This story is a parable about fulfilling the true nature of marriage.

The *Catechism* deals with chastity and purity in its treatment of both the Sixth and Ninth Commandments, and we will follow its direction.

Chastity is both an attitude and an act. The Ninth Commandment, which speaks of purity of heart, dwells on the chaste attitude. The Sixth Commandment focuses more on chaste behavior, reasons for it and ways to achieve it. All people are called to be chaste in the sense that human sexuality should be integrated into the full humanity of the person and not considered just a physical act.

> Chastity means the successful integration of sexuality within the person and thus the inner unity of man in his bodily and spiritual being. Sexuality, in which man's belonging to the bodily and biological world is expressed, becomes personal and truly human when it is integrated into the relationship of one person to another, in the complete and lifelong mutual gift of a man and a woman. (CCC, 2337)

The sexual act may only be performed within a marriage. Married people are expected to be chaste inasmuch as their sexual behavior is in a context of mutual self-giving and reverence for each other's human dignity. It also implies that the spouses will not seek other sexual partners outside the marriage. To avoid confusion, it must be noted that celibacy, whether for single people or for those who have taken a vow, is not the same as chastity. But at the same time, celibates are obliged to be chaste, avoiding lust or a sexually active life.

In any discussion of chastity, we should begin with the truth that the body is sacred. It is a temple of the Holy Spirit. "Do you not know that you are the temple of God and that the Spirit of God dwells in you?" (1 Corinthians 3:16). Both Scripture and the Church honor the holiness of the body.

Church teachings about sex and chastity originate with a reverence for sexuality and the flesh. God created the body and sex, and both have come from his hand as good. Hence we do not start with hostility to the flesh or a fear of sexuality. Both of these are gifts of God intended to participate in the acts of salvation and contribute to our quest for holiness.

This needs to be understood since there have been periods of history in which there were movements that looked with suspicion, fear and hostility to sex and the body—and it could happen again. This was true of Manicheism, Albigensianism, Puritanism, Jansenism and Victorianism.

Chastity is a form of loving because it is a characteristic of authentic marital love. Chastity does not stifle the heart. On the contrary, chastity channels the sexual act, and its attendant emotions, toward the full surge of the heart in conformity to God's will and the good of the spouse.

Husbands and wives expect to love and care for one another. This means they will have to view each other as persons and not things, as centers of human dignity. Chastity becomes beneficial here because it cancels lust, which would cause the spouses to use one another for self-gratification instead of productive love.

Freedom is often spoken of as the capacity to choose good and evil, and this is true. But we should also add that the choice for evil lessens the ability to be free, is an abuse of freedom, while the selection of good makes us more free. Freedom is not a static experience.

We will make progress in freedom the more we act in

conformity with God's plan for our happiness and salvation. The choice for chastity will give married people a deeper experience of freedom and the same can be said for celibates, dedicated singles and adolescents going through their developmental stages.

Self-Mastery

Chastity requires *training in self-mastery*, which gives us a proper experience of human freedom. Either we govern our passions and find inner harmony and peace or we let ourselves be ruled by our emotions and drives and become unhappy. Free people are not slaves of passion.

Chastity is identified with the cardinal virtue of temperance, reflecting the self-restraint that we need to avoid immoral behavior. People have always known that a virtue is necessary for being moral. The virtue of chastity grooves into our soul the behavior that will free us from immoral sexual acts and liberate us for sexual activity that promises both human fulfillment as well as a sense of freedom we all crave.

> There are three forms of the virtue of chastity. The first is that of the spouses, the second that of widows, and the third that of virgins. We do not praise any one of them to the exclusion of others.... This is what makes the richness of the discipline of the Church. (Saint Ambrose, *On Widows*, 4, 23)

Temptations to lust arise from within us as well as from the seductions from other people or from obscene films, music, books, plays, pictures or stories. If I want to remain faithful to my baptismal promises, I must use the means to do so. I must know myself, adopt a suitable asceticism, obey God's commandments, practice moral virtues and be fervent in prayer.

Self-mastery is a demanding, lifelong project. We can never be sure we have won the battle. "The effort required can be more intense in certain periods, such as when the personality is being formed during childhood and adolescence" (*CCC*, 2342). Our task is made easier when the culture supports us. Conversely, our success will help us change and improve the culture. Our chastity is a grace, a gift from God and a result of spiritual effort.

The *Catechism* lists the following sins against chastity: lust, masturbation, fornication, pornography, prostitution and homosexual acts (cf. *CCC*, 2351-2359).

In its discussion of homosexuality, the *Catechism* acknowledges the existence of sexual attraction between some members of the same sex. It has taken a variety of forms throughout history, and its origin remains largely unexplained.

While opposing homosexual acts as intrinsically disordered and against scriptural teaching and the natural law, the *Catechism* calls for just treatment of homosexuals. "They must be accepted with respect, compassion and sensitivity. Every sign of unjust discrimination in their regard should be avoided" (*CCC*, 2358).

Homosexuals are called to chastity, self-mastery and the gift of inner freedom. Admittedly, this is a challenge for them. There is a Catholic ministry to homosexuals called Courage. Its mission is to assist them to live chastely and provide them with communal support within the context of prayer, meetings and openness to the graces of God.

While admitting the urgency of the sexual issues related to the Sixth Commandment, what is at stake is a person's capacity to be permanently faithful to a spouse and to family responsibilities in marriage. This drive to fidelity arises from the experience of love between a man and a woman, both in its romantic beginnings and in the second wind of marriage.

God has planted the drive to fidelity in the middle of every love relationship. Marriage is the best way to fulfill that drive; the body and sexuality should be its servants. Moreover, God offers an example of faithful love.

Everyone knows that fidelity presents an awesome

challenge to married people. Yet those who know the considerable joys of such fidelity and those who have met couples blossoming in its sunlight find plenty of inspiring evidence that the challenge can be met. Fidelity is not only one of life's greatest satisfactions, it is also a taste of God's love for us.

For Dialogue

1) This chapter argues that the body and sexuality are fundamentally good. How well does this ring true in your experience? Do you know people who seem to have undue anxiety and guilt about their bodies and their sexuality? What are the possibilities of restoring the ideal of chastity in our culture?

2) Romantic lovers tend spontaneously to make enthusiastic promises of mutual constancy. What application does this have for the value of fidelity? Do passing crushes and infatuations invalidate the lessons about fidelity that romanticism generates?

3) Why is it true to say that fidelity is the central value supported by the Sixth Commandment? How would you help teenagers to say no to sex until they are married? Your sister and her husband have been unable to have children in 14 years of marriage. They have decided to try in vitro fertilization. How would you respond to the news of their plans?

Meditation

Here are three pointers that every family can practice to create the chaste counterculture:

1) *Thou shalt dress modestly.* There is a way to remain fashionable and modest at the same time. People speak of the "classic cut" that survives amid all the vagaries of fashion. Hence this suggestion is not meant to make

family members look like "Miss Early America of 1912." Clothing makes a statement. If our clothes are intentionally seductive, then a wrong signal is being given. If they are quietly modest, whether formal or informal, then the signal is, "I respect you; I respect myself."

2) *Thou shalt listen to good music.* This can include pop music and modern musical forms as well as the classics. Music sends powerful emotional messages. Why not listen to that which enhances love without immediate sexual gratification; music that inspires us to treat each other as persons and not objects of violence and degradation, music that is romantic without bullying the young into premature relationships?

3) *Thou shalt save sex for marriage.* Virginal purity in both men and women is an attainable ideal. It was done by cultures for centuries. It can be done again. There is nothing so new about our culture that it automatically demands the breakdown of morality. Cultural changes have occurred time and time again. Permissiveness has often accompanied such changes in the past. But people came to their senses and returned to the classical religious and moral virtues. We are not helpless. We are simply being sold a bill of goods that we do not have to buy.

Prayer

Father in heaven, you are the author of marriage and willed that the covenant of husband and wife should reflect the covenant you have established with us. Your beloved son willed that the covenant of marriage should reflect his own union with the Church. In these events, the virtues of fidelity and chastity are paramount, Christian ideals that assure the stability of the family and look to the welfare of children. We ask for all the virtues, gifts and blessings we need to fulfill these Christian ideals of marriage and the family. AMEN.

Love each other or perish. (from *Tuesdays With Morrie)**

*Mitch Albom, *Tuesdays With Morrie* (New York: Doubleday, 1997), p. 149.

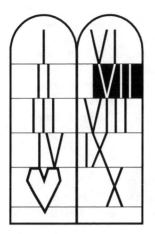

CHAPTER SEVEN

Seventh Commandment

Don't Steal—
Act Justly

You shall not steal.—DEUTERONOMY 5:19; MATTHEW 19:18

I Gave the Money Back

Last Sunday night, I found myself without a place to stay. So needless to say my financial position is a little tight right now. Last night I went through a drive-through restaurant. When paying for the order I handed the woman a five-dollar bill. She gave me change for a twenty-dollar bill. I pulled forward to get my food and then putting the money away I realized I had over fifteen dollars. At this point I was faced with a little dilemma.

I sure could have used the extra money, and after all, it wasn't my mistake right? Wrong. I pulled out of the parking lot—I want you to know I could hear you, Dr. Laura, in my head—nagging. Then I saw the cashier in my head. She was not real young. Probably had kids and probably making half my meager wages. A till that was short of fifteen dollars could be a real problem to her. I turned around and went back—parked my car and walked up to her window.

She looked nervous—probably thinking I was there to complain. When I handed her fifteen dollars and said, "I think you gave me too much change," she didn't know what to do. Once the look of disbelief left, then came the look of great relief, and finally she was able to mutter, "Thank you." I want you to know that the look on her face was worth fifteen thousand to me. I felt better about everything in my life after that. I cannot describe the sensation it gave me. (Dr. Laura Schlessinger, *The Ten Commandments: The Significance of God's Laws in Everyday Life* [New York: Harper-Collins, 1999], 253)

The thief must no longer steal, but rather labor, doing honest work with his [own] hands, so that he may have something to share with one in need. (Ephesians 4:28)

Do You Believe Stealing and Injustice Are Wrong?

The *Catechism* presents these instructions on respect for others' property and the call to seek justice for those in need:

- Respect people and their possessions (page 126).
- Learn and practice the Church's social teachings (page 130).
- Be a steward of the goods of creation (page 137).

- **RESPECT PEOPLE AND THEIR POSSESSIONS**. (CCC, 2401-2425)

There is plenty of stealing going on.

Armed robbery, from simple street muggings to heists at automated teller machines, remains the most prevalent crime that Americans should fear from strangers. Robbers strike 1.2 million times a year, injuring their prey about a third of the time. Eighty-four percent of robberies are committed by strangers. One in 20 cases results in serious injury and lost property.

Beyond these instances of stealing are numerous cases of white-collar crime, embezzlement, computer theft, counterfeit money, fraud, mail scams and many other inventive ways of theft. People are worried about their safety and the security of their possessions. They want stronger police protection and bigger jails for the offenders. They are wiring their homes with alarms, moving into guarded gate communities and even hiring personal bodyguards.

God's laws forbid stealing.

> The Seventh Commandment forbids *theft*, that is, usurping another's property against the reasonable will of the owner.... Even if it does not contradict the provisions of civil law, any form of unjustly taking the property of others is against the Seventh Commandment. (CCC, 2408-9)

In Old Testament society, most people had very few possessions. They depended on the little they owned for subsistence and survival. Most had no savings. They had no state-supported safety net against starvation, homelessness or sickness.

A robber who took a winter robe exposed the victim to freezing. The predator who stole a small flock from a shepherd in a hand-to-mouth economy could ruin a family. When people owned only tiny bits of the Earth's surface (as billions of people in the Third World still do), a theft of property could be devastating. One's precious few possessions were "sacred" indeed when one's life and family survival depended on them.

Biblical law expected thieves to make restitution. An apprehended thief was expected to do more than merely return what was stolen: "When a man steals an ox or a sheep and slaughters or sells it, he shall restore five oxen for the one ox, and four sheep for the one sheep" (Exodus 21:37). If the thief could not pay, he was to be sold into slavery to pay for his theft. Generally speaking, the law required a thief to pay at least twice the value of what he stole, and occasionally even five times.

One is responsible for protecting one's neighbor's goods from accidental loss:

When a man is burning over a field or a vineyard, if he lets the fire spread so that it burns in another's field, he must make restitution with the best produce of his own field or vineyard.... When a man gives money or any article to another for safekeeping and it is stolen from the latter's house, the thief, if caught, must make twofold restitution. (Exodus 22:4, 6)

The biblical assumption is that one has a right to own property, and that one's rights should be respected.

As the incidence of stealing has risen in our society, there are a number of initiatives to counter this problem.

There is renewed interest in the restoration of moral and character education in our schools and churches. This is a form of preventive medicine that will raise a generation of young people who would internalize the virtues of honesty and respect for persons and property.

Relevant to this approach is the *Catechism's* advocacy of the excellent *virtues of temperance, justice and solidarity.* Temperance restrains our inclination to greed. Justice teaches us proper regard for the rights of others and their property. Solidarity with all humans instructs us in the beauty of the golden rule, "Do unto others as you would have them do unto you."

Armed with these virtues, we can appreciate better why theft is wrong: because it is the usurping of another's property against the reasonable will of the owner. Included here would be fraud, paying unjust wages, forcing prices up by taking unfair advantage of another.

"The following are also morally illicit: work poorly done; tax evasion; forgery of checks and invoices; excessive expenses and waste. Willfully damaging private or public property is contrary to the moral law and requires reparation" (CCC, 2409). This list is not meant to be exhaustive, but indicative of failures in responsible stewardship as well as loss of respect for persons and their possessions.

The restoration of trust and community would help diminish the various forms of stealing. Trust grows when people experience trustworthy human beings. Fortunately, a good many people do have experiences of honest behavior. We hear heartwarming stories of someone returning a lost wallet, money intact, to the owner. We hear of a gas station owner who accidentally left his pumps on all night and found that every motorist who used them left money, and of a farmer who runs a retail store on the honor system and testifies that his customers are honest to a fault.

That spiritual power is still present and available in cities and towns. The leaders of all religions are newly aware of their responsibility for nurturing the communal hungers of their people and becoming the glue for new forms of gathering in a disparate society. Ecumenical and interfaith movements have created networks in which they can together cooperate for safe neighborhoods and provide their people with the spiritual experience of God's trustworthiness.

The Seventh Commandment's challenge to trust has a compelling relevance today. Its ideal of trust is meant to liberate people from the many forms of human venality, from stealing a bar of soap to cheating a widow, from insider trading to wasteful cost overruns for weapons, from shoplifting to redlining, from indifference to the world's poor and hungry to the raping of earth, air and water.

Life Application

1) If you have been mugged and robbed, what impact did it have on your life? If your home has been burglarized, what have you done about your house? In these cases, what insights have you gained about the Seventh Commandment?

2) How does a trusting community make stealing less possible? What are ways that such communities can be established in what has been called a "nation of strangers"? Why would the restoration of moral and character training in our schools and churches be a

valued strategy in rolling back the tide of theft?

3) The Church teaches that Scripture calls us to be responsible stewards of the goods of the earth. What are some ways we can practice this stewardship? How might it reduce stealing?

- **LEARN AND PRACTICE THE CHURCH'S SOCIAL TEACHINGS.** (*CCC*, 2419-2436)

    Some years ago an assassin was hired to kill Dom Helder Camara, the late archbishop of Refice and Olinda in northeast Brazil. The executioner came to the door of his simple wooden home and knocked on the door.

    A very small, frail-looking man opened the door.

    Speaking with authority, the visitor said he wanted to see Archbishop Camara.

    "I am Dom Helder," replied the little man at the door.

    His image of the archbishop instantly shattered, the assassin stammered, "You are Dom Helder?"

    "Yes," answered the 'red bishop' as many called him. "What do you want? Come in. Do you need me for anything?"

    "No, no," said the assassin, clearly flustered. "I don't want to have anything to do with you because you are not the kind of man one kills."

    "Kill? Why would you want to kill?" asked Dom Helder.

    "Because I was paid to kill you, but I can't kill you," the assassin replied.

    "If you are paid, why don't you kill me?" the archbishop reasoned. "I will go to the Lord."

    "No," said the assassin. "You are with the Lord."

    And he got up and went away. (Vicky Kemper with Larry Engle, "A Prophet's Vision and Grace," *Sojourners* [December 1987], 12)

This retired archbishop remained a shining example of

Christ's love and a tireless worker for the Church and a world that follows Christ's way of justice, love, mercy and peace. Dom Helder taught that the world will be changed and God's will shall be done through the faithful, persistent efforts of small groups of people who "hope against all hope."

Dom Helder witnessed the values of the Seventh Commandment in which God calls all of us to create a just society, a peaceful world, a respect for human dignity and a stewardship of the goods of the earth, which makes this possible. He was the living embodiment of the Church's social doctrine.

> The social doctrine of the Church developed in the nineteenth century when the Gospel encountered modern industrial society with its new structures for the production of consumer goods, its new concept of society, the state and authority, and its new forms of labor and ownership. (CCC, 2421)

Cure the Causes of Poverty and Injustice

We are called to heal the causes of injustice and poverty. This summons us to examine how business, government, education, medicine and other social forces affect the helpless in our society and in the poor countries of the world. This is a complicated task and demands our working together with like-minded people in a common cause. Solutions are not easy and never swift, but that should only challenge us all the more.

Catholic social teaching embraces both Catholic social tradition and an *explicit* Catholic social doctrine. The *social tradition* has been part of Church life since her beginning and includes the inheritance of social consciousness embodied by Genesis and the prophets and the social concern of the People of God of the Hebrew covenant.

In its simplest form it calls for the curing of the causes of poverty and injustice.

Social doctrine refers to the teachings of the popes, councils and bishops dating from Pope Leo XIII's *Rerum Novarum* in 1891 to the present day.

The *Catechism* contains several treatments of the Church's social doctrine in different sections. Read paragraphs 355 to 421 for the *Catechism*'s understanding of what it means to be a human being, the origin of human dignity, the problem of the Fall and the promise of redemption. In the simplest of terms, we learn that we are radically flawed by original and actual sin—and radically redeemed by Christ's saving death and resurrection.

Next, look at paragraphs 1897 to 1948, where the *Catechism* deals with our participation in social life, the role of authority, the importance of the common good, social justice and human solidarity. Finally, read paragraphs 2401-2449, the *Catechism*'s treatment of the Seventh Commandment, most of which pertains to the Church's social doctrine.

This wonderful body of teaching deserves lengthy and prayerful study and meditation. To live the Church's social doctrine demands of us humility and love for the poor. We speak of this as curing the symptoms of poverty and injustice. When we have a personal involvement in the needs of the poor and unjustly treated, then we are made more open to the call to seek social justice for them.

Dom Helder Camara and Mother Teresa exemplified the twofold approach of healing the causes and symptoms of poverty. Camara witnessed social justice; Teresa labored one-on-one with the symptoms of poverty. Both were humble servants of God. When asked how he handled applause and fame, Camara told the following story.

> I remember when Mother Teresa and I were at the 1976 Eucharistic Congress in Philadelphia. One of the major TV studios invited us to appear for a fifteen-minute segment on national television. When I arrived at the studios, Mother Teresa was already there.
>
> She said, "Oh, Dom Helder, I remember how beau-

tifully you described the way you protect yourself when you enter an auditorium filled with people who are giving you a standing ovation, how you pray, 'Lord Jesus, this is your triumphal entry into Jerusalem. I'll be your little donkey.' I don't have the courage to call myself Jesus' little donkey. Because of my experience in India, I'm going to pray, "Let me be your old cow."

So I said to Mother Teresa, "Let us pray the prayer of Cardinal Newman together." When I got to the end I added, "May your grace so cleanse and envelop us that people's eyes may not see only Dom Helder and Mother Teresa, but may see through our lowly human presence and discover your divine presence. Take away whatever is opaque in us and help us become transparent." ("A Prophet's Vision and Grace," 17)

"Those who are oppressed by poverty are the object of *a preferential love* on the part of the Church which, since her origin and in spite of the many failings of her members, has not ceased to work for their relief, defense and liberation through numerous works of charity which remain indispensable always and everywhere." (CCC, 2448)

When her mother reproached her for caring for the sick and poor at home, Saint Rose of Lima said to her: "When we serve the poor and the sick, we serve Jesus. We must not fail to help our neighbors, because in them we serve Jesus."

On his death bed, Saint Vincent de Paul was asked by a novice what was the best way to deal with the poor. "You must love them, sister. Then they will be able to forgive you for the bread you give them."

Saint John Chrysostom said this about ministry to the poor: "Not to enable the poor to share in our goods is to steal from them and deprive them of life. The goods we possess are theirs, not ours" (Homily on the Parable of Lazarus and the Rich Man).

Jesus teaches us, "Whoever has two cloaks should share with the person who has none. And whoever has food should do likewise" (Luke 3:11). Saint James reinforces this truth, "If a brother or sister has nothing to wear and has no food for the day, and one of you says to them, 'Go in peace, keep warm, and eat well,' but you do not give them the necessities of the body, what good is it?" (James 2:15-16).

Acts of real love for the poor are the best way to start living the Church's social teachings. There is no substitute for personal contact with those who need our help. We are called to heal the *symptoms* of poverty and injustice. A loving ministry to the poor, the hungry, the naked, the vulnerable and marginalized is the best way to fulfill this vocation.

The Story of Amos

No one preached this message more cogently than the prophet Amos. Born in Tekoa around 750 B.C., this rustic mountaineer passed his days taking care of his sheep and his sycamore grove. He never dreamed of being a prophet, but once the Lord called him, he approached the task with customary brusqueness.

Amos was the first of the great reforming prophets. As a genuine social critic, he fumed at people's disregard for even the simplest standards of decency. The self-indulgence of the rich enraged him. They slept on ivory beds, gorged themselves on lamb and wine and smelled of expensive perfume while treating the poor unjustly and ignoring their basic human needs.

The rich cushioned their consciences by participating in worship and practicing ceremonial pieties. They used religious practice as an excuse for not having social concern. Nothing shamed them. Amos derided their hypocrisy with God's words:

> I hate, I spurn your feasts,/I take no pleasure in your solemnities..../But if you would offer me holocausts,/then let justice surge like water....(Amos 5:21, 23b-24a)

Amos was not opposed to liturgy itself but to immoral people who use worship as a cloak for their malice. Majestic music and rituals are no substitute for moral living. His eye was on the heart, not the ceremony. He fought for a religion that included the quest for justice.

Amos focused his ministry on the royal sanctuary at Bethel and its local community. Bethel was enjoying a booming economy due to windfall from several successful wars. The merchant princes were living high. In the golden glow of this prosperity, people could scarcely believe that the doom predicted by Amos would really happen.

Amos faced a tough audience, but he knew how to get their attention. He did not mind being rude. The day he addressed the local women's club as "cows of Bashan" (4:1), he dispelled any illusion that he would employ tact and diplomacy to communicate his message.

He was no expert on international affairs, but Amos knew about a powerful Assyrian neighbor. He understood how moral decadence and active exploiting of the poor was the normal prelude to impending disaster. He warned the business leaders, "Your wife shall be made a harlot in the city,/and your sons and daughters shall fall by the sword..." (7:17). Those prosperous burghers thought Amos a religious crank, a rustic figure of fun shouting foolish doomsayings. Spoiled children mocked him in the streets, aping his mountain twang and unsophisticated ways.

Eventually, the city leadership tired of him and persuaded Amaziah, pastor of the royal chapel, to get rid of this pest. Amaziah developed a spurious treason charge and used it to exile Amos: "Off with you, visionary...never again prophesy in Bethel; for it is the king's sanctuary and a royal temple" (7:12a-13b).

Amos gave the world one of the first documents of social protest. He identified with the poor and unjustly treated. He proclaimed an ethical God who is affronted by worshipers who use religion to rationalize injustices.

Rough-hewn as he was, Amos loved his people and

took no pleasure in the doom that awaited them. He scourged the people because he loved them, just as God did. He wept over them because they loved neither God nor the poor who needed their enlightened compassion.

Amos initiated a consciousness about social justice that one great prophet after another continued. Jesus stood firmly in that prophetic tradition by announcing that his gospel would be good news for the poor. His unforgettable parable about the rich man and Lazarus (Luke 16:19-31) illustrates that a redemptive covenant with God includes noticing poverty and doing something about it.

Justice is stewardship in action. Where the people stood in faith depended on how they treated one another with justice—especially for the most vulnerable in society. This prophetic message is as important for the twenty-first century as it was in the tenth century B.C.

Jesus continued and enlarged the teachings of Genesis and the prophets. Jesus perfectly embodied what it meant to be an image of God (cf. Colossians 1:15) and an ideal steward of the earth's goods. Of his many rich teachings, his "sheep and goats talk" best reflects the prophetic concern for the marginalized, the hungry, the thirsty, the naked, the prisoners, the sick, the unjustly treated (Matthew 25:25-40).

Like the prophets, Jesus turns our attention to the widow, orphan and alien, those at the edge of the circle. Like him, we should also care for those at the edge: the poor single-parent mothers, the host of illegitimate children, the vast army of refugees, homeless and others who need our love. The goods of the earth are not just for us and our families but for all humanity.

We need to be convinced that justice, mercy and love are possible for all human beings. We must combine our human ingenuity with a reliance on the grace of God to effect a conversion of mind and heart in those institutions and leaders who need it so they can join us in bringing the fruits of the Kingdom of God into our world.

We have an abundant supply of biblical and Church teachings to guide us. What we could use is an army of Christian witnesses, working together with all people of goodwill to accomplish the ideals of justice and love for every person on earth.

Growing in Faith

1) What are some Scripture texts that motivate you to love the poor and to help change factors that keep them poor?

2) How can the Church's social teachings help us deal with the problems of poverty in our society and the world?

3) What is the best way to learn how to love the poor and to have a preferential option for the poor?

Growing in Knowledge

1) How would you undertake a systematic study of the social teachings of the Church?

2) What can you do to instill the virtues of temperance, justice and solidarity in your own life and the next generation of young people?

3) What impresses you about the witness of Archbishop Camara and Mother Teresa?

• BE A STEWARD OF THE GOODS OF CREATION.
(CCC, 2415-2418)

When Cardinal Stafford was head of the Denver archdiocese, he took a two-week drive through the Western Slope of Colorado, a region known as "God's country." He saw squalor and misery in the valleys and exploding affluence on the peaks.

"I saw large mansions on the sides of the mountains, luxurious homes that are empty most of the year. In the valleys, I saw colonies of trailer parks where the working people live, often without adequate heating and basic services. This is wrong. Something is awry."

He spoke out in a 12-page pastoral letter titled *The Heights of the Mountains Are His: The Development of God's Country.* He identified the problem as a hyperdevelopment of a playland for the privileged at Aspen and Vail, along with a growing underclass of workers who earn the lowest wages in the hotels and restaurants and can scarcely afford a decent roof over their heads.

He pleaded with employers and government to promote social and economic justice in the region—as well as to address the ecological crisis in the mountains, parks, valleys and rivers. He asked them to be true stewards of creation, a calling that has a firm biblical foundation.

The Genesis account of creation communicates both the value of the created world and the dignity of man and woman as images of God. As images of God, we are called to be stewards of creation. The world is "God's farm," and we are the farmers. The Church teaches that the "universal destination of the goods of the earth" is for the common good. Stewards know this and act responsibly for this goal. (Read Genesis 1:28-29; 2:15.)

Care for Creation

The old Puritan axiom claimed that cleanliness was next to godliness. If that be so, then there is not much godliness in our environment. Our ancestors' "waste not, want not" attitude has surrendered to the wasteful attitude of the industrial nations. The failure to treat nature responsibly—burning coal, wood and oil, which fill the sky with carbon dioxide gases that trap heat—is causing a greenhouse effect that may melt the polar ice cap and threaten the existence of coastal cities.

Disrespect for nature also thins the ozone layer, releasing the sun's harmful ultraviolet rays. This increases the risk of skin cancer, disrupts the process that causes plant growth—and therefore threatens the food chain. Waste dumped into oceans and rivers threatens the water and fish supply.

In the Book of Genesis, the Creator established the value of environmental responsibility. The principle is related to being an image of God. God told humans to have dominion over the world with its birds, fish and animals. God placed the first humans in the Garden of Eden and instructed them to image God by tilling the earth and taking care of creation.

To image God is to take moral responsibility for creation and one another, to treat the cosmos and each other just as God does: with positive regard for persons and all creatures. To image God is to treat the earth and its waters as centers of goodness that require care, concern and a bias for harmony and peace.

The first creation story (Genesis 1:1—2:4a) displays a loving and creative God who brought harmony out of chaos. The second creation story (Genesis 2:4b—3:24) tells the sad tale of human beings who managed to draw chaos out of the harmony they received as a gift. In our age, when environmental sensitivity means so much, this biblical teaching is more relevant than ever. If we are truly imaging God, our treatment of creation will be more responsible and respectful.

Local communities can do something about waste dumping once they have the will to pay for it and the imagination to find new ways to control it. Many communities have initiated separate garbage pickup for recyclable trash, thus reducing by half the waste disposal problem. Another community has created an enclosed pond for sewage. In time, the bacteria clean the water, which is then released into another reservoir where an artificial lake serves as a nature sanctuary.

Public policy and international agreements are needed to clean the air of carbon dioxide and fluorocarbons. This will mean finding ways to reduce use of gasoline, raising fuel-efficiency standards for cars, increasing budgets for solar research and safer nuclear energy sources, and banning some products.

The trees are the lungs of the earth, yet 28 million acres of forests are destroyed in the Third World every year. The United Nations has proposed that foreign debt be swapped for forest conservation. For example, American banks and Brazil could forge an agreement in which Brazilian debt service would be reduced by so many millions of dollars in return for conserving thousands of acres of rain forest. Reforestation programs would help purify the air of carbon dioxide and provide fuel for Third World countries.

Christian moral training should instill in the young and in adults alike a healthy respect for nature, an understanding of the potential disasters that lie ahead and a sense of community responsibility for the care of the earth.

Conclusion

The Seventh Commandment's value package of trust encompasses honesty, justice and environmental responsibility. It provides an inspiring challenge for all people of goodwill and should also stimulate a covenant renewal among all Christian believers. God has led the way as a resoundingly trustworthy partner, continually raising up prophets for the cause of justice and sustaining a cosmos that will work in our favor if we follow nature's laws. God has modeled how the Seventh Commandment should be understood and observed.

In Jesus Christ, this becomes transparently clear. Jesus betrayed no one. He is the supreme exemplar of trust. By his saving work in the cross and resurrection, Jesus has provided us with both the example of trust and the supernatural grace that makes it possible in all those who respond to him in faith. The challenge exists. The grace is available. Now must come the joyful response of faith.

For Dialogue

Several years ago, a firm commissioned a barge to transport its garbage to a country willing to accept it in return for a fee. No country could be found. The "garbage barge" roamed the seven seas like a polluted Flying Dutchman. The nightly news carried the story and taught us about one of our environmental problems. The smog alerts in our major cities presage the coming disasters of the greenhouse effect. The growing incidence of skin cancer informs us about a disintegrating ozone layer.

1) How do we develop our consciences to see this as a moral issue as well as a legal one?

2) What are similar examples you could raise from your experience?

3) Who are people you know who have acquired environmental awareness?

Meditation

If human vices such as greed and envy are systematically cultivated, the inevitable result is nothing less than a collapse of intelligence. A man driven by greed loses the power of seeing things as they actually are, of seeing things in their roundness and wholeness, and his very successes become failures. If whole societies become infected by these vices, they may indeed achieve astonishing things, but they become increasingly incapable of solving the most elementary problems of everyday existence....

I suggest that the foundations of peace cannot be laid by universal prosperity, in the modern sense, because such prosperity, if attainable at all, is attainable only by cultivating such drives as greed and envy, which destroy intelligence, happiness, serenity, and thereby, the peacableness of man. It could well be that rich people treasure peace more highly than poor people, but only if they feel utterly secure—and this is a contradiction in terms. Their wealth depends on making inordinately large demands on limited world resources and thus puts them on an unavoidable collision course—not with the poor (who are weak and defenseless) but with other rich people.

No one is really working for peace unless he is working primarily for the restoration of wisdom (E. F. Schumacher, *Small Is Beautiful* [New York: Harper-Collins, 1989]).

Prayer

Generous Father, you have placed us at the table of abundance that is the goods of the earth. You have taught us that all these goods are meant for the benefit of every human being. You also give us the right to private property so our families can live in human dignity and have the stability we need for achieving proper goals here and eternal life hereafter. At the same time, you call our attention to the needs of the poor and helpless. They are our brothers and sisters and need our generosity and concern. Fill us with the courage and wisdom to keep their needs before us and do what we can to help them. AMEN.

Any system in which social relationships are determined entirely by economic factors is contrary to the nature of the human person. (Pope John Paul II, *Centesimus Annus, 24*)

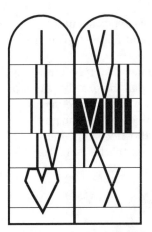

CHAPTER EIGHT

Eighth Commandment

Tell the Truth

You shall not bear false witness against your neighbor.
—DEUTERONOMY 5:20

Do not take a false oath.—MATTHEW 5:33

If My Son Lies...

My little boy is seven now but I have handled the issue of lying in a way that has helped in his early years and is still working. I've consistently stressed to him that if he tells the truth—he doesn't get punished. Of course I will find out or see if he is lying so I will know what is a lie or what is the truth. He might get a stern talking to and lecture, but no punishment.

If I find out that he has lied then there is punishment which has taken the form of sending him to his room to "think about his actions," me manifesting a nonunderstanding and exasperated mood and expressing my strong dissatisfaction, no treats, or whatever seems appropriate at the age.

It has never really got to any real punishment because it has worked quite well. Positive reinforcement about truth telling in his early years—regardless of the severity of the action—has worked. I have told him that telling the truth is sometimes the hardest thing and that we always will have to talk about it (no real getting off?), but that he should not be fearful of the ramifications of truth telling.

Even now, when I ask him things like if he threw his lunch away or ate it, he will tell me exactly why and what he threw away and what he ate. Sometimes, it takes a little coercion and a reminder of the "no punishment for truth" rule, but the decision almost always is to avoid the P word. Hope this helps. (Letter from a mother)

Do You Believe in Telling the Truth?

The *Catechism* highlights these ways of acquiring the virtue of truth telling:

- Live, witness and respect the truth (page 144).

- Get rid of deceit (page 149).

- Enjoy the beauty that truth brings (page 153).

- **LIVE, WITNESS AND RESPECT THE TRUTH.**
  (*CCC*, 2464-2474; 2488-2492)

We proclaim the ideal of telling the truth, with our hand upon the Bible in every courtroom: "I swear to tell the truth, the whole truth and nothing but the truth." We talk of truth in lending, truth in advertising, truth in our relationships. But we are not strangers to deception and lying. Deep down we realize the truth is often lacking.

We believe our personal lives and our society would be better and happier if we lived in the truth. The Eighth Commandment summons us to live, witness and respect truth.

There is an African legend about the eternal struggle between truth and falsehood.

Years ago, Truth, Falsehood, Fire and Water were traveling through the countryside. They came upon a herd of cattle with no one to look after it. They discussed this and concluded that the most reasonable thing to do would be to divide the herd into four parts, giving each an equal share.

Privately, Falsehood plotted to get it all for himself.

Calling Water aside, Falsehood said, "Fire plans to burn the grass along the riverbanks and drive the cattle away from you into his pasture. I advise you to extinguish him now and we can have his share of the cattle for ourselves."

Water gullibly listened to Falsehood and flooded Fire and extinguished him.

Now Falsehood whispered conspiratorially to Truth, "Water has destroyed Fire and plundered his cattle. You and I don't want company such as his. Let's take all the cattle and climb the mountain."

"Come back!" said Water, who could not follow them because he could not go uphill.

At the mountaintop, Falsehood laughed at Truth, "I have fooled you. Give me all your cattle or I will crush you."

Truth replied, "So, you have deceived me, but I will never be your slave."

With that they began to fight fiercely. Each time they clashed, thunderclaps shook the earth and sky. No matter how violently they smashed against one another, neither could prevail. Eventually, they called upon the Wind to settle their contest.

"I cannot judge a winner here," said the Wind.

Truth and Falsehood are destined to struggle. One time Truth will win; another time, Falsehood. Truth must always recover, get up again and fight until the end of the world. Truth must battle Falsehood and never rest or surrender; otherwise Falsehood would prevail. That is why eternal vigilance and courage is necessary for the final victory of Truth.

Honesty and truthful living are the bedrock of a functioning society. People cannot live together if no one is able to believe what anyone else is saying. Truth is essential to trust. God has put into all human beings the drive to seek and expect the truth and to respond to the challenges that truth demands. In the Eighth Commandment, God calls us to be committed to truthful living and to resist all temptations to deceit. The Catechism offers us a framework for re-sponding to God's call to tell the truth and battle falsehood.

> Truth as uprightness in human action and speech is called *truthfulness*, sincerity or candor. Truth or truthfulness is the virtue which consists in showing oneself true in deeds and truthful in words.... The disciple of Christ consents to "live in the truth," that is, in the simplicity of a life in conformity with the Lord's example, abiding in his truth. (CCC, 2468, 2470)

In his story *Gulliver's Travels*, the satirist Jonathan Swift asked the question, "Why would anyone be dishonest?" He has Gulliver meet a group of people who were so rational they found deceit beyond comprehension. One of them explains to Gulliver, "The use of speech was to make us understand one another and to receive information and facts. Now if anyone said the thing that was not [that is, lies], these ends were defeated."

They believed that lies would have no place in a world that was inhabited by totally reasonable people. Unhappily, people are not in fact fully rational. We possess a fund of passions, impulses, drives and tendencies that do not easily harmonize with reason. We need practice and study over a long period of time to acquire the habit of truthfulness and honesty. We also need faith, prayer and grace to acquire the virtue of truth.

History is full of stories of people who valued the truth so highly they were willing to die for it. Saint John Fisher surrendered his life rather than approve of King Henry VIII's divorce or deny the truth that the pope is Christ's appointed head of the Church. Franz Jagerstatter refused to accept the big lie of the Nazis, and he was martyred for his commitment to the truth of Christ. During the French Revolution, a convent of Carmelite nuns bravely went to the guillotine rather than bow before the goddess of reason or abandon the truth for which their vows stood.

Jesus Confronts Pilate With Truth

In the trial of Jesus before Pilate, it is clear how central the matter of truth is. When Jesus heard the lies that were spoken about him from his enemies, he responded, "For this I was born and for this I came into the world, to testify to the truth" (John 18:37).

In the presence of Pilate, Jesus stands for the most important of all truths, the necessity of salvation from sin. Truthful living, therefore, not only makes us people of integrity; it also transforms us into a saved people. Just as lies make a hell for people on earth, so do truths introduce the glimpses of heaven and prepare us for eternal life.

The encounter between Jesus and Pilate shed the full light of day on the inherent attractiveness of truth and the dignity of Jesus who witnessed it. Truth triumphed at the Antonia palace despite the shameful behavior of the politician Pilate who glibly washed his hands of responsibility for Christ's death.

Pilate's skeptical question, "What is truth?" broods like a cloud over modern society. Today's skepticism flattens all statements into opinions. This creates a value vacuum and a loss of confidence in the knowability of truth. Self-destructive people will take over a culture where the truth tellers are silent. The Irish poet William Butler Yeats described this in his poem "The Second Coming":

...the center cannot hold....
The best lack all conviction, while the worst
Are full of passionate intensity.

Truth is understood by study, love and practice. Study alone is not enough, for in such a case, truth remains an abstraction and its full meaning is not grasped. Truth must move to the heart and to behavior before its genuine potential is appreciated. Logical acceptance of truth is only a third of the story. There must also be love of the truth.

The heart must engage truth every bit as much as the mind. Why? Because truth is more than simply an idea. Truth contains beauty, attractiveness, the unifying power of love. The mind sees truth as an idea. Love beholds truth as a revelation of beauty, ultimately even of God. Why else would Jesus have said that he not only possessed the truth but was indeed the living revelation of truth?

Lastly, the insight into truth demands living what truth stands for. Truth belongs to a triad: to know, to love, to act. Once truth is known, loved and lived, then its magnificent promise is realized. One of the main reasons skepticism and relativism have prevailed in our culture is these attitudes influenced people to think of truth as only an idea divorced from the loving and living steps. When this happened, truth, held only as an idea, withered before the onslaught of the "marketplace of ideas" where opinions counted more than truth.

The Church insists that truth is more than correct objective thoughts; it is the object of our love and passion, and it is the dynamic motivation for our behavior. Intelligence, love and behavior all disclose the many splendored reality of truth. Know the truth. Love the truth. Live the truth.

Reflection

1) How did your parents teach you to tell the truth? In what way do their lessons abide in your adult life? What has been your experience in teaching children and others to be truth tellers? How strong has been your influence and witness?

2) What happens to a family when truth is in short

supply? What is the effect upon society when truth is not considered an essential virtue? How do stories that emphasize the value of truth telling help train us all to avoid lies?

3) When is it hard to speak the truth? Why do moralists point out that for every lie we need to be ready tell more lies? What is the connection between truth and trust?

- **GET RID OF DECEIT.** (*CCC*, 2475-2487)

Saint Augustine defined lies as sins because they misuse God's gift of speech. It is not always easy to detect a lie. Matters would be simpler if liars' noses, like Pinocchio's, grew each time they told a lie. Successful lies, by definition, go undetected. All lies have one thing in common: the intention to mislead, to conceal, to falsify.

Lies may confuse the hearers, but liars know exactly what they are doing when they tell untruths. Lies come in many shapes and forms. Mark Twain, not too seriously, claimed there were 869 forms of lying. Most likely, there are as many kinds of lies as there are liars.

The *Catechism* lists the following types of behavior as reprehensible forms of lying: false witness, perjury, rash judgment, calumny, flattery or adulation that confirms another in malicious or perverse conduct. In all these cases, we have lying with the intention to cause harm to others.

Lying not only hurts other people; it also corrupts the one who lies, as well as undermines the trust that is the basis of a wholesome society.

The mass media, which has acquired such enormous influence in the shaping of public opinion and communicating information, should remember its responsibilities of justice, charity and truth.

As users and consumers of the mass media, we should overcome passivity in the face of this flood of information. We should be vigilant about what is directed to our children.

This means we must form enlightened consciences so that we can more easily resist unwholesome influences upon ourselves and our families. The tide of negativity, half-truths and taste for scandal that characterizes portions of the mass media and entertainment industries creates a mood of cynicism in those who passively take it all in with no moral filter to judge its potential for corruption.

Each of us must be convinced that truth works better than lies for the health of the family and society. Journalists and entertainers who get beyond the urge to shock, scandalize and exploit sex and violence for its appeal to our baser natures will find they can do more for society by simply telling the whole truth in a wise and prudent manner.

The credibility of rulers strengthens their capacity to rule. Business managers who want an enthusiastic workforce have much more going for them when they are honest and open with their people. Spouses show how much they really love one another when they are truthful with each other.

Truth works better than lies because it corresponds to the drive that God put in our human natures for our happiness and self-realization. Truth produces the kingdom of love. Deceit releases self-destructive impulses.

Truth makes us really free. The more people practice truthful living, the greater is their inner sense of liberation. This is not achieved easily nor quickly. The process of truthful living demands a lifetime of struggle and moral courage. Those engaged in this process experience it as worthwhile. Their remarkable sense of inner freedom testifies to us that truthful living is its own reward.

Honor People With the Gift of Truth

Truthful people have the interests of humanity at heart. They will move technology toward positive use in society. Truthful living demands dedication to the search for truth and determination to stick to it and live by its liberating gift. Truth is not coerced but is granted as a gift to a faithful seeker.

Liars murder more than the truth. They kill souls and they often cause physical death. Hitler revealed his agenda when he said in *Mein Kampf* that the big lie works even better than the small one. Hitler's lies about the superiority of the Aryan race and the supposed danger posed by the Jews led to the Holocaust and the worst war in history.

Jesus proclaimed divine truth, but he also showed how intimately human dignity is bound to truthful living. Is not honestly searching for truth, responsibly meditating upon it and joyfully accepting its meaning for life one of the greatest treasures of the human spirit? Truth has a divine aspect. Truth—science, art, literature, wisdom and conscience—also belongs to human knowledge.

Jesus calls every human being to witness to the truth. We should not conceal truth or deny it to others. That is the real meaning of our Lord's words, "Your light must shine before others, that they may see your good deeds [your truthful living] and glorify your heavenly Father" (Matthew 5:16). Humans have the right to know the truth. Too much energy has been wasted in thinking of reasons why people should not be given the truth.

Saint Paul frequently admonished his people to avoid lying:

> Stop lying to one another, since you have taken off the old self with its practices and have put on the new self, which is being renewed, for knowledge, in the image of its creator. (Colossians 3:9-10)

> ...you should put away the old self of your former way of life, corrupted through deceitful desires,...and put on the new self, created in God's way in righteousness and holiness of truth. Therefore, putting away falsehood, speak the truth, each one to his neighbor, for we are members one of another. (Ephesians 4:22, 24-25)

Paul's language about taking off the old self and putting on the new one refers to the baptismal liturgy. The candidates removed their clothes and were submerged into the baptismal waters. When they came out of the water, they donned new white robes, which signified the inner change caused by Christ's saving grace. Plunged into Christ through faith and grace, the candidates emerged as new people, expected to begin a new moral and spiritual life in Christ. Incorporated into Christ, the head of a new humanity, the candidates shared in the power of his Holy Spirit.

Paul considered this baptismal experience motivation to live an honest and truthful moral life, since the candidates belonged to humanity renewed in Christ. Behaving in an honest way toward one's sisters and brothers in Christ was a sign that Christians appreciated what their new existence demanded. To lie was to act unfaithfully to a member of Christ's Body. Paul's words applied Christ's own teaching to the question of moral conversion: "...whatever you did for one of these least brothers of mine, you did for me" (Matthew 25:40b).

Life Application

1) In the spring of 1963, Pentagon spokesman Arthur Sylvester became the center of controversy when, defending his actions during the Cuban missile crisis, he asserted that the government had the "right to lie" in its own defense. Twenty-five years later, former White House spokesman Larry Speakes wrote in *Speaking Out* that he lied in order to polish the president's public image. Does the government have the "right to lie" in a crisis or to boost a president's image? When citizens find out a government is lying, what happens to their attitudes toward public officials? What would a society where everyone lived truthfully be like?

2) A forty-six-year-old woman goes to her doctor for a

routine physical checkup. The doctor discovers she has an inoperable cancer that will kill her in six months. Chemotherapy may prolong her life a few months, though it will have painful side effects. The patient feels well and plans a vacation. What should the doctor do: tell his patient the truth, deny it if asked or delay telling her until after the vacation? Should the doctor conceal the information about chemotherapy? What should a nurse or medical student who knows about the case say to the patient?

3) Jesus witnessed to truthful living throughout his career and accepted suffering and death as part of the price. How have you imitated Christ's commitment to truthful living in your own experience?

• ENJOY THE BEAUTY THAT TRUTH BRINGS. (CCC, 2500-2513)

In its final section on the Eighth Commandment, the *Catechism* expounds an inspiring connection between truth and beauty, in both its natural and divine forms. Here is a link between truth and art, between truth and the contemplation of the beauty of God in the act of wisdom. As images of God, we are able to know the truth, desire goodness and form a community of love with one another.

But being God's images also includes expressing the truth of this relationship in works of art. The ability to create a work of art in music, poetry, dance, sculpture, painting, architecture, drama, opera, oratorios and other forms is a uniquely human act.

Beyond our daily workload, our efforts to provide for our families and their future, we have the capacity to create and appreciate art and beauty, which is an extraordinary flowering of our inner riches. Art emerges from a talent given by God and is developed by human effort, training, discipline and lengthy dedication. True art reveals the truth of God and life through a wide range of expressions that appeals to our intuition and ministers to our hunger for beauty.

> The fine arts, but above all sacred art, "of their nature are directed toward expressing in some way the infinite beauty of God in works made by human hands. Their dedication to the increase of God's praise and of his glory is more complete, the more exclusively they are devoted to turning men's minds devoutly toward God." (*CCC*, 2513)

True sacred art draws us to adore and love God. It is the gift of wisdom that inspires this quest for beauty and also moves us into a contemplative mood where our prayer and appreciation of the wonder of God come together. Both the artists and the contemplatives are opened to the truth of God through the emanation of wisdom.

> [Wisdom] is a breath of the power of God; and a pure emanation of the glory of the Almighty.... For she is the reflection of eternal light, a spotless mirror of the working of God, and an image of his goodness....I became enamored of her beauty. (Wisdom 7:25-26; 8:2, *New Revised Standard Version Bible*)

Religion and art have generally been mutually useful to one another. Countless artists have used their talents to reveal the beauty of God to the world. Sacred art—and its visible results in cathedrals and monasteries and parish churches—contains thousands of examples of how truth as God's wisdom has nurtured faith through the centuries. Let us drink at the fountain of truth in all its blessed forms.

Conclusion

In Shakespeare's *Hamlet*, when young Laertes is about to leave home and embark on his career, he asks his father, Polonius, for guidance. His dad delivers a series of practical proverbs that have proved to warrant the good life. Then he tells his son:

This above all: to thine own self be true,
And it must follow, as the night the day,
Thou canst not then be false to any man.

In other words, "Be an honest man, my son." Polonius knew the value of truthful living. The Eighth Commandment invites us all to the same discovery.

Growing in Faith

1) How would truthful living give you an experience of inner freedom?

2) How do you feel when you have been deceived? How does this help you avoid deceiving others?

3) Why is it important not only to know the truth but also to love it and live it?

4) Who is the most honest person you know? What are you learning from this model of truthfulness?

Growing in Knowledge

1) How would your experience of beauty help you know the truth—and even know God better?

2) What can you do to increase the trust factor in your family, your circle of friends and your local community?

3) What should be done to influence government and the mass media to be more committed to truth and trust building?

4) What are some stories about telling the truth in difficult circumstances that you could share with others?

Meditation

Telling the truth is something which must be learned. This will sound shocking to anyone who thinks that it must all depend on moral character and that if this is blameless the rest is child's play. But the simple fact is that the ethical cannot be detached from reality, and consequently continual progress in learning to appreciate reality is a necessary ingredient in ethical action. In the question with which we are now concerned, action consists of speaking. The real is to be expressed in words. That is what constitutes truthful speech. And this inevitably raises the question of the "how?" of these words. It is a question of knowing the right words on each occasion. Finding this word is a matter of long, earnest and ever more advanced effort on the basis of experience and knowledge of the real. If one is to say how a thing really is, i.e., if one is to speak truthfully, one's gaze and one's thought must be directed towards the way in which the real exists in God and through God and for God." (Dietrich Bonhoeffer, "What is Meant by Telling the Truth?," *Ethics*, ed. Eberhard Bethge [New York: Macmillan, 1965], 363-372)

Prayer

Holy Spirit, give us the gift of truth telling. Show us how to speak the truth with simplicity of heart. Remind us that trust is the glue that holds our family, friends and society together. Help us meditate on Jesus, who both taught the truth and embodied it in his life. Instill in us the moral courage that will make truth an act of integrity in our daily behavior. AMEN.

Tell the truth and shame the devil.

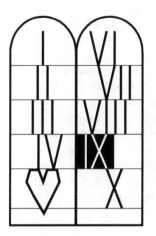

CHAPTER NINE

Ninth Commandment

Happy Are the Pure of Heart

You shall not covet your neighbor's wife.... —EXODUS 20:17

Everyone who looks at a woman with lust has already committed adultery with her in his heart. —MATTHEW 5:28

The Company One Keeps...

Marie knew Tim was "It."

"Tim was the Man," said Marie. "The one I will marry."

Marie was an honor student, elected to the executive council of her sorority, little sister for a fraternity, and an active member of the Inter-Varsity Christian Fellowship. Both Christians, she and her boyfriend had a wonderful "warm caring relationship. We would pray and have Bible studies together."

As their relationship progressed, his fraternity brothers and her sorority sisters could not believe that they were not sleeping together. Still, Marie was extremely wary. Most of her girlfriends, including most of her Christian girlfriends, already had succumbed to the temptation of sex. They were tormented by guilt and remorse, some panicked by the possibility of pregnancy.

"After crying with them and loving them through

these times, I realized that nobody was immune. I was almost terrified. If it can happen to them, it can happen to me."

So how did Marie do it: manage to remain chaste through four years of college and going steady? "God blessed me. I prayed a lot before going to college and He put me on a hall with at least three other girls as committed as I was. I draw heavily from my friends for guidance and support and invest my life with the people I live with. It was very important that the first thing I did was to get involved with Christian women." (Kimberly R. Bucher, *Crisis* [September 1993], 37)

Are You Resolved to Live a Chaste Life?

The *Catechism* invites you to consider these principles for a chaste lifestyle.

- Live in intimacy with the Holy Spirit (page 158).

- Practice purity of heart (page 162).

- Let the gospel shape your attitude to sex (page 167).

• LIVE IN INTIMACY WITH THE HOLY SPIRIT. (CCC, 2514-2516)

"If we live in the Spirit, let us also follow the Spirit" (Galatians 5:25). In Baptism and Confirmation, we are given the gift of the Holy Spirit. This person of the Trinity is associated with the pure and infinite love of the Father and the Son.

Since sex is intimately linked with the possibilities of love, it would seem that the invitation to walk with the Spirit is the best way to place sex in its proper context. The popular mind equates having sex with making love. Certainly this would be true in marriage, where sex is permitted and the spouses have a reverence for each other's integrity. Married couples who walk with each other and abide in the Spirit of love are in tune with God's plan for their lives and have the chance of breathing in a continuous stream of love from God.

We have already reflected on the Sixth Commandment, which shows us how our sexual behavior in the context of marriage provides the couple with unitive love and procreative fruitfulness.

The Ninth Commandment draws our attention to the interior attitude of purity that should govern our vision of sex and love. Taken together the Sixth and Ninth Commandments offer us the divine plan for sex, love and marriage.

Since the Ninth Commandment focuses on the spirituality of love and sex, it seems best to benefit from the active presence of the Holy Spirit in our bodies and souls. What does this quest for a spiritual gift of purity entail? It makes us aware of our passions and desires and the decisions they present to us. It is all too evident that we are often inclined to desires that are contrary to the love the Spirit wants to give us. Instead of love, we choose lust.

The Ninth Commandment calls us to choose pure love and put away impure lust. It awakens us to the inner drama of our emotions, thoughts and drives. If we walk with the attitudes promoted by a sexually permissive culture, we will most likely not be chaste. If we journey with the ideals of purity deeply flowing from the loving Spirit, we will know the secret of chastity and its real promise of love.

When Saint Paul went to Corinth, he found a culture that had wandered far from the life-affirming purity that the Spirit plants in every man and woman through the natural law. The expression "to live like a Corinthian" meant following an "anything goes" philosophy in sexual matters; a "Corinthian girl" was a call girl.

The sailors who thronged to this busy port worshiped Aphrodite, from whom they hoped to gain good luck in their sexual adventures. Her temple dominated the city from a 1,700-foot cliff. One report said she had a large number of priestesses serving her—and also servicing the local male population. Aphrodite (called Venus by the Romans) presided over a cult in which sex was the object of worship. Today's cult of the body as a sex object has similar religious overtones. Greek and Roman artistic portrayals of the old goddesses degenerated into pornography just as in present society.

It was hard for Corinthian men and women to remain chaste in their society, just as today's women and men are challenged by modern permissive culture. In his First Letter to the Corinthians, Paul gives an extended treatment of the virtue of chastity. His exposition adds more light to the biblical appreciation of the meaning of the Ninth Commandment. The text reveals the kind of objections to chastity that Paul encountered—arguments that sound like those raised by the defenders of the new morality.

Paul heard them say, "Everything is lawful for me" (1 Corinthians 6:12). In other words, morality is determined by the individual without any reference to a divine law. Each person decides for himself what is moral. Morality is just a matter of choice. Choosing makes it right "for me." This is an approach to moral decision making all too common today—often on issues of sexual behavior.

Paul came across another slogan, "Food for the stomach and the stomach for food" (1 Corinthians 6:13), meaning that sex is as natural as eating and should be just as free from moral laws. Paul could have heard the same line from a prominent modern promoter of the new morality, Bertrand Russell, who wrote in *Marriage and Morals* that "Sex is a natural need, like food and drink." It may be a natural need, but like all such needs, it must be understood as under the direction of a human person.

Paul's response to these Corinthian arguments arose from his Christian vision of a human being. Consistent with the theme of the clean heart that gives one the vision of how God looks at human behavior, Paul is able to see the truth of the matter. Sexual activity would be no different from eating and drinking if humans were no more than animals.

Animals satisfy their physical needs and have bodies that live and die and disappear. But human beings have bodies that are destined for resurrection. Jesus Christ has sanctified and consecrated the human body, Paul argued. "The body...is not for immorality, but for the Lord, and the Lord is for the body; God raised the Lord and will also raise us by his power" (1 Corinthians 6:13-14).

Baptism makes it possible for a Christian body, female or male, to be united mysteriously with the Body of Christ. Therefore, to sin sexually with such a body is to make sacrilegious use of Christ's Body. This is what Paul meant when he wrote, "Do you not know that your bodies are members of Christ? Shall I then take Christ's members and make them the members of a prostitute? Of course not!" (1 Corinthians 6:15).

In Baptism, Christ anoints a person's whole body with the Holy Spirit as the priest seals this event with the oil of chrism. In Baptism, the body becomes holy with the holiness of the Spirit. The new Christian shares in both body and soul the very being of Jesus Christ. That is why the proper use of sexuality becomes the source and means of holiness.

Paul's memorable explanation of the value of chastity applies just as well today as it did for the Corinthians. This vision of the body is possible for the clean of heart who begin from the viewpoint of seeing God and experiencing divine love. True chastity never pretends sex does not exist or that there is something degrading about it. Real chastity is not ashamed of the body. It provides the baptized with the opportunity to glorify God in our bodies.

Chastity is the virtue by which we impose self-control on our sexual life so that it will not be used for make-believe loving but will be reserved for the true pledge of love in marriage. Chastity puts love into lovemaking. A chaste person accepts sexuality from God with gratitude and uses sex as God intended for spreading love in the world.

Life Application

1) How conscious are you of the scriptural teaching that your body and soul are temples of the Holy Spirit? If you were more aware of this divine presence, given to you at Baptism and Confirmation, what would it mean for your spirituality and your attitude to sex, love and marriage?

2) How have you developed your inner attitudes to sex and love from adolescence to the present? Who had the deepest impact on your progress? How have you been shaped by the teachings of Scripture and the Church? How strong has been the position of the culture on these matters?

3) If you believe you are in need of inner renewal on matters of sexuality, what would you be seeking? How would you guide young people today to adopt the Christian vision of sex and love and marriage?

• PRACTICE PURITY OF HEART. (CCC, 2517-2519)

Many people confuse chastity with celibacy, probably because the vow of celibacy taken by members of religious orders is called the vow of chastity. But chastity is not about the absence of sexual activity. Chastity is about a clean heart, whether one is married or celibate. Chastity should be as present in the act of intercourse as it is in the vow to abstain from sex.

Chastity is best understood when one appreciates what Scripture says about the clean of heart. In the Old Testament, ritual cleanness guaranteed access to the temple, not just because one had taken the ritual baths but because the bodily cleanness symbolized a clean heart. The soul needed to be clean as well as the body:

> Who may go up the mountain of the LORD?
> Who can stand in his holy place?
> The clean of hand and pure of heart.... (Psalm 24:3-4a)

When Isaiah envisioned God's glory at the temple, he felt his heart was too unclean to be there. He said he was a man of unclean lips, meaning that he did not feel he had the undivided heart, the kind of directness one should have when it came to the things of God. As he hungered for such a pure inner attitude, an angel came with a burning coal and touched his lips. The divine fire transformed Isaiah. The angel assured him: "See,...now that this has touched your lips, your wickedness is removed, your sin purged" (Isaiah 6:7).

The biblical ideal of a clean heart means that one should have a one-track mind when it comes to God, for it is in the heart that decisions are made. Jesus told some of the Pharisees that they spent too much time on religious and moral externals. They looked at deeds and failed to notice intentions. They measured moral goodness by correct behavior and did not contemplate the motives. They should probe deeper and examine the state of the heart. Jesus taught them that the sins against the commandments originate in a misdirected heart:

> For from the heart come evil thoughts, murder, adultery, unchastity, theft, false witness, blasphemy. (Matthew 15:19)

In the Bible, heart language is decision language. It has to do with motives and intentions. A clean heart is not mixed. Jesus knew his listeners associated the word clean with washed clothes, with corn that had the chaff winnowed out of it, with an army purged of inefficient soldiers. It could also mean wine unmixed with water, or pure, unalloyed metal. Jesus was saying that people should have hearts whose motives were not mixed but turned arrow straight toward God.

People see only what they are able to see. Ordinary people who gaze at the stars from a hillside at night will see a thousand points of light. If they happen to be astronomers, they will know stars and planets by name. If they are sailors, they will pick out the stars that are used to navigate a ship. Acquired skills and professional training enable people to see what they have been educated to perceive.

Clean hearts give people the capacity to see God—that's why Jesus wants people to acquire them. People with clean hearts have one-track minds about love, which draws them to God. It is love that does the seeing; love reveals Love. That is why the Bible locates the purity of a love decision in the heart.

How does chastity fit in with this biblical vision of a clean heart? A person who has an undiluted love for God is able to transfer the experience into genuine love for another. True love would not dream of exploiting the relationship. A pure love for another person excludes all thought of a utilitarian relationship, be it useful for financial, political or sexual reasons.

Because chaste people enjoy loving God in simplicity of heart, they are able to love another with the same wholehearted enthusiasm. If they are celibates, they will love without seeking a sexual fulfillment. If they are married, they will signify their love by sexual union and express their affection. A clean heart makes the difference because, being able to see God and experience a loving union with the divine, the motive for loving another person is never mixed with selfishness or derailed by disordered passions. The core of the union resides in the heart; hence the state of the heart must be examined with utmost care.

David and Bathsheba

The Bible tells a tale that illustrates the absence of a clean heart in a relationship: the story of King David's passion for

Bathsheba. She is a married woman; nonetheless, David seduces her. When she later tells him that she is pregnant due to the liaison, he brings back from the front her soldier husband, Uriah, hoping that their marital union will cover up the situation.

To his surprise, the husband refuses to have sex with his wife because he believes that a soldier should remain celibate while his comrades are in the heat of battle. David orders him back to the scene of the fighting, entrusting him with a letter to his commanding officer. The letter gives instructions to place Uriah where he is most likely to be killed.

The plan succeeds and Uriah dies. David marries Bathsheba. The baby is born but becomes desperately ill. The prophet Nathan confronts David with his adultery and murder. With matters out of control and his world crashing around him, David admits his sins and repents, hoping both for forgiveness of his sins and for the healing of his child. God forgives his sin, but the child dies.

In his psalm of repentance, David does not talk about adultery or murder. He does not list his woeful behaviors. He talks about his heart because he knows that is where the real trouble lies. He knows perfectly well that adultery and murder are terrible acts, but he realizes it is far more important to get at the heart of the matter:

> A clean heart create for me, God;
> renew in me a steadfast spirit.
> Do not drive me from your presence....
> Restore my joy in your salvation....
> (Psalm 51:12-13a, 14a)

Behavior modification, useful as it may be, will not solve David's problem. He digs deeper and asks for a conversion of heart. He believes that God can make this happen, so he pleads for the creation of a clean heart. His new heart will bring him three things: a steadfast spirit, a constant union of love with God and the joy of salvation.

The steadfast spirit means one that willingly remains fixed on God. Remaining always in God's presence assures a permanent growth of love between oneself and the Lord. The result of all of this is an experience of redemption and its consequent joy. David asks God for profound personal renewal and correctly believes that God is as interested in bringing this about as he is in praying for it. God gladly heard David's prayer.

God solved for David the problem of his disordered passions by creating a new heart for him. David heard again the sounds of joy and gladness. His sense of remorse had made him feel as though his bones were crushed. Now that he had a new heart, his "crushed bones" rejoiced. God had washed not his body but his heart.

Reflection

1) The challenge of chaste living requires the support of the Church community as well as God's grace. What suggestions would you offer someone to gain God's help and acquire self-control for chastity? What would you say to someone who claims that unchastity is not the worst of sins, for there are many worse forms of immorality?

2) Read 2 Samuel 11—12:25, the story of David's lust and repentance. David's lust led him to adultery, a cover-up and murder. How true to life is this story? What should David have done when he first saw Bathsheba? Would you have used Nathan's confrontational approach to David? If not, what would you do?

3) What people in your life have inspired you by their purity of heart? How have they come to this attitude? What have you learned from them?

• LET THE GOSPEL SHAPE YOUR ATTITUDE TO SEX. (*CCC*, 2520-2531)

Sex is a strong passion, but not a blind instinct. Humans can control it. Despite many teachings to the contrary, self-control is the road to real freedom, while free love abandons self-control and makes sex the slave of passion. Sexual license is clearly the opposite of freedom. Chaste living implies control of thoughts and desires as well as behavior. Jesus was quite direct on this issue: "But I say to you, everyone who looks at a woman with lust has already committed adultery with her in his heart" (Matthew 5:28). A chaste person practices modesty and lives a lifestyle that reflects a commitment to purity.

Christ calls everyone to practice chastity: priests, religious, those getting ready for marriage, married people and single persons. Jesus summons each person to purity of mind and heart in fidelity to one's vocation. Happily, a multitude of witnesses in every age of Church history, including the present age, have integrated chaste expressions of their sexuality and love into fulfilling and rewarding lives.

Those who resolve to live chastely have decided to love as Jesus did. Chaste love is more interested in giving than taking. In its most noble form, it will even draw one to die for the beloved.

Two conflicting invitations challenge the minds and hearts of contemporary women and men. The erotic society sends its insistent messages about love without responsibility and unfettered sex without guilt. Jesus sends an invitation to honor purity and love chastely. A permissive culture basically lies to its constituents, promising them happiness and contentment by means of free love and irresponsible sex. Jesus tells the "truth in love" (Ephesians 4:15) and the truth about love.

The Ninth Commandment contrasts inner attitudes about sexuality. On the one hand, it speaks against lust, just as Jesus did in his Sermon on the Mount. Positively, it extols the virtue of chastity as Jesus did in the Beatitudes: "Blessed are the clean of heart, / for they will see God" (Matthew 5:8).

For some time now, to speak of chastity has been considered unfashionable. If religious people attempt to offer chastity as a positive value, they often face a hostile reception. Some people think that one should never talk publicly about sex or chastity. Their upbringings have made them think there is something shameful about the topic; they are embarrassed if chastity is mentioned, since one would also have to treat the dreaded sex topic.

Other people do not want to hear about chastity because they figure the Church is just trying to impose a guilt trip on them, to emphasize fear of human sexuality and identify every sexual act and thought as sinful. They often contend that the Church is interested only in sexual immorality, not any other kind.

Church leaders and ministers would be the first to admit that defective preaching, teaching and guidance among some religious leaders has presented an inadequate view of sexuality on occasion. But in all fairness, it should be admitted that such presentations proceeded from a belief in the sacredness of sex and the holiness of the marriage state. Besides, past mistakes ought not to deter a present commitment to communicate a positive and inspiring teaching on sexuality and chastity.

Such is the spirit of the Irish bishops in their pastoral letter *Love Is for Life:*

> God created our sexual being in his own image, created it for goodness and loveliness. Christ redeemed it for grace and gracefulness. The presence of grace in sexual love makes it, quite literally, "graceful." The absence of grace from sexual love makes it, quite literally, "dis-graceful." Marriage is ordained by God to make sexual love graceful.
>
> Firmly convinced that human weakness can be overcome when affection for Jesus becomes a priority in one's life, the Church bears Christ's message to all

who are willing to listen. The Church offers the compassion of Jesus for those involved in sexual sins, making the forgiveness of God, who is "rich in mercy" (Ephesians 2:4), available in the Sacrament of Reconciliation.

A Gospel Response to the Culture

Contemporary society is marked by the sexualization of consciousness. TV is largely responsible for this because it has so pervasive an impact on so many people. A senior in high school will have spent 25,000 hours watching TV— about as much time as in the classroom. TV presents to young and old alike a continuous stream of love stories where vivid sexuality—often immoral—is portrayed. Seldom do the stories probe the spiritual aspects of the relationships. The ideal of being clean of heart is virtually nonexistent in these presentations.

Advertising gives most Americans 3,000 "shots" a day. A great many ads use seductive sexuality to attract the viewer to the product. Thus sex is exploited for sales. The sexualization of awareness reaches its worst form in the dehumanizing impact of prostitution, pornography and so-called adult entertainment centers. Businesses based on the exploitation of sex contribute to degradation, especially of women and children.

Parents, priests, catechists and counselors should respond to the sexualization of consciousness by the spiritualization of awareness. We all need to place the concern for chaste living prayerfully in our hearts. A faith perspective is the proper context for the quest for a clean heart. This quest will include loving support, counsel and study. It will mean encouraging anyone who seeks to be chaste to be in touch with the sacramental life of the Church, Reconciliation and the Eucharist above all.

The Church calls Catholics to be signs of contradiction for an erotic society, after the example of Jesus Christ.

Motivated by his love for each human being, the Redeemer died on the cross and rose from the dead to save us from our sins. Even when we fall into sin, Christ's love never ceases. He reaches out to us in forgiveness. Our repentance invites the divine grace that strengthens our resolve to be chaste.

Not only the grace of Christ but also the prayers and example of the Blessed Virgin Mary accompany us on the challenging and rewarding journey of chastity. Mary, the Ark of the Covenant, reveals the glory of Jesus. We behold in Mary the beauty of chastity and its reward. What makes her chastity so appealing is its revelation of Christ's glory and the outstanding love that flowed from her chastity. Mary's religious faith assumed a concrete form in her life of love, a love that is the essential counterpart of true chastity for us all.

Mary identified with her beloved. Real love motivates the lover to live in the mind of the beloved and to be possessed by the heart of the beloved. True love seeks the bond of affection. The difference between prostitution and love is that in the former there is union of bodies but not unity of persons, whereas in the latter there is a unity of both.

God asked Mary to love him so much that there would be identification between lover and beloved. Since Mary had always remained clean of heart, she knew how to answer the call. Her faith statement was, "May it be done to me according to your word" (Luke 1:38b). Mary chose to be one in mind and heart with God. Then she received the inexpressible gift of identification in body.

The Ninth Commandment confronts us with the question, "What is the state of your heart?" Jesus tells us the best answer would be that our hearts are clean. That is the secret of chastity. That is the loving message that helps us to see God and live morally satisfying lives.

For Dialogue

1) Discuss the issue of sex education. What are its advantages and disadvantages? How closely should parents be involved?

2) Explore the possibilities of training people in chastity, for singles, people in vows and married people.

3) Debate ways in which the gospel can be applied to culture in a constructive manner.

Meditation

Is abstinence a realistic expectation? Yes and no. No, if the expectation is that all youngsters will wait until marriage before having sex. Yes, if it means that a majority can be persuaded that postponing sex is the right thing to do. It is true that some will "do it anyway." It is also true that actual behavior tends to fall below the cultural ideal. What this means in practice, however, is that the higher the cultural standard is set, the farther actual behavior rises to meet it. In turn, the lower its standard, the farther below it actual behavior will sink.

Once the standard falls to the level of recreational sex—about where it is now—we shouldn't be surprised to find that exploitative sex has become the norm for many, or that date rape has become a major problem. (William K. Kilpatrick, *Why Johnny Can't Tell Right From Wrong* [New York: Touchstone Books, 1993])

Prayer

Holy Spirit of love, walk with us in our quest for purity of heart. Enlighten our minds to see the beauty of chastity. Strengthen our will power so that we can resist the temptations to lust. Calm our unruly passions and redirect them to positive goals. Show us how to be obedient to your creative will for our human growth, development and the goal of eternal life. AMEN.

To the clean all things are clean. (Titus 1:15)

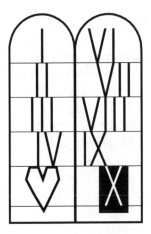

CHAPTER TEN

Tenth Commandment

Banish Greed and Help the Poor

You shall not desire your neighbor's house or field... nor anything that belongs to him.—DEUTERONOMY 5:21B

For where your treasure is, there also will your heart be.
—MATTHEW 6:21

Who Is the World's Happiest Person?

Once upon a time in Asia, there lived a man named Croesus, the world's richest man. One day he received a visitor named Solon, a lawmaker from Athens. He was considered the world's wisest man. Croesus showed Solon his grand rooms, the fine carpets, the soft couches, his gardens, orchards and stables—and the thousands of rare things he purchased with his gold.

That night at dinner, Croesus asked his guest, "Tell me, Solon, who do you think is the world's happiest person?"

"I think it was a poor Athenian, called Tellus."

"Why so?"

"Tellus worked hard all his life. He used all his money to give his children a good education. When they were grown, he joined our army and died defending our homeland. Could anyone be happier?"

"Perhaps not. But who would rank next to him in happiness?" Croesus kept thinking that Solon would say, "Croesus."

"Well there is the case of two young men whose father died when they were children. They were very poor. Still, they worked hard to support their mother who was in ill health. Year after year they toiled with no thought of anything but their mother's comfort. When she died they gave their whole love to Athens and served the city until they died."

"Why do you make no mention of my wealth and power? Why rank these poor working people above me, the world's richest man?"

"My friend, no one can judge how happy you are until you die. No one knows what misfortune will overtake you and how you will react."

Some years later, a powerful king, named Cyrus, arose and conquered the kingdom of Croesus. The soldiers plundered all his wealth and planned to burn him at the stake. Cyrus was passing by at that moment and heard the old king yelling, "Solon! Solon!"

Cyrus stopped and spoke to Croesus. "Why do you call for Solon?"

Croesus then told him the story of Solon's visit.

Cyrus pondered Solon's words. "No man knows what misfortune may overtake him and what misery will be yours in place of all this splendor."

Cyrus said, "Should not we be merciful to those in distress? I will do to Croesus as I hope others will do to me if I face misfortune."

He freed Croesus and treated him as one of his most honored friends.

Do You Have an Unhealthy Desire for Material Goods?

The *Catechism's* reflection on the Tenth Commandment presents these thoughts for a proper attitude to money and possessions:

- Examine the state of your heart (page 175).

- Learn the option for the poor from the story of Saint Francis (page 180).

- Be generous and remove disordered desires (page 187).

• EXAMINE THE STATE OF YOUR HEART.
(CCC, 2544-2547)

The opening story about Croesus and Solon is adapted from the writings of the Greek historian Herodotus. Croesus was the king of Lydia in Asia Minor from 560 to 546 B.C. It is of interest to us here because the wise Solon identified self-sacrifice and generosity as keys to happiness.

When we examined the Seventh Commandment, we looked at the outer behavior of people, the ways they can respect others' property and avoid stealing, and the actions they should take on behalf of social justice by healing the symptoms and causes of poverty and injustice.

Now in the Tenth Commandment, we concentrate on the inner thoughts, desires and attitudes that people have about money and possessions.

When Jesus began the Sermon on the Mount, he outlined a series of eight spiritual attitudes that would make us happy. The first of these stated that poverty of spirit would enable us to inherit the kingdom of God. In other words, the road to real happiness begins with a healthy detachment from material goods.

Later on in this same sermon, Jesus taught that building up material wealth for its own sake is foolishness. We should be more interested in spiritual riches.

Do not store up for yourselves treasures on earth, where moth and decay destroy, and thieves break in and steal. But store up treasures in heaven, where neither moth nor decay destroys, nor thieves break in and steal. For where your treasure is, there also will your heart be. (Matthew 6:19-21)

When Jesus saw a poor widow put her tiny contribution into the temple treasury, he praised her for having a generosity greater than all the others, who gave out of their abundance, while she gave from her meager resources. She was not simply poor; she had poverty of spirit.

Jesus went on to tell the story of a rich man who owned a great farm and built a grand new barn. He piled up his wealth and planned to eat, drink and be merry for many years. Jesus quotes God as saying, "You fool, this night your life will be demanded of you; and the things you have prepared, to whom will they belong? Thus will it be for the one who stores up treasures for himself, but is not rich in what matters to God" (Luke 12:20-21).

And then remember the dialogue between Jesus and a young rich man:

> "Teacher, what good must I do to gain eternal life?..."
>
> "If you wish to enter into life, keep the commandments...."
>
> "Which ones?..."
>
> "You shall not kill; you shall not commit adultery; you shall not steal; you shall not bear false witness; honor your father and your mother; and you shall love your neighbor as yourself...."
>
> "All of these I have observed. What do I still lack?..."
>
> "If you wish to be perfect, go and sell what you have and give to [the] poor, and you will have treasure in heaven. Then come, follow me." (Matthew 19: 16-21)

When the young man heard Christ's solution for possessing the joys of eternal life, he went away sad, for he owned a lot of material things. It was at this point that Jesus noted the spiritual difficulty people have who are attached to their possessions. Jesus said that it would be easier for a camel to go through the eye of a needle than for such people to enter God's kingdom.

The Rich Get Richer

Not only do people attached to money fail to understand how to get to heaven, they often cause misery here on earth for those who are poor. As a popular saying puts it, "The rich get richer and the poor get poorer."

The TV show *Who Wants to Be a Millionaire?* asks a question to which millions say "Yes, I do." The hunger for quick wealth abounds in our society. Young computer wizards are making millions, even billions. Youthful day traders are moving into monster homes in gated communities. The older rich are finding shelter in pricey Park Avenue condominiums. In one case, not untypical, a company wanted to oust its chief executive officer. The bargaining resulted in his getting a deal in which he would receive five million dollars a year until he died—and, his wife would then get three million dollars a year until she died. The "golden parachutes" (exit benefits for many CEOs) are shining brighter than ever.

The rich are getting richer. The result is inequality in our society and a greater sense of lostness among those at the bottom of the pile. In 1979 the top five percent of people earned ten times more than the bottom twenty percent. In 1999 the top five percent earned nineteen times more than those at the bottom. It used to be said that when the water rises all the boats rise together. What was not said is that all the boats do not rise equally. Inequality is greater than ever.

And this does not even speak to the gap between rich nations and poor ones. Pope Paul VI drew our attention to the North-South problem in our world, in which the nations of the northern regions of the world need to acquire a social conscience regarding the poorer nations of the southern regions. He spoke of the need for a progress of all countries (*Progressio Populorum*).

Now, it is not the purpose of this brief chapter to outline the Church's teachings on social justice for all peoples. We have already explored some of these in our lesson on the Seventh Commandment. Nonetheless, it is important to allude to the current problems that are raised by the mad scramble for material wealth caused by the technological revolution (computers, the Internet, communications). The issues of greed and avarice and conspicuous consumption should be on the minds of all who hold the gospel vision of a wholesome detachment from material goods.

Saint Paul writes that the love of money is the root of all evils (cf. 1 Timothy 6:10). Money itself is not the problem. The "love" of money is the real question. Greed is the evil that causes both misery for the poor and spiritual emptiness for the rich. Right now we have a giant "morality play" unfolding before us. We are witnessing a modern gold rush that matches any in history—and all the old sins that come with it are up front for all to see. Making money in unimaginable sums is where the action is. But just wait for the reaction. No, do not wait.

This is a time to recover the simplicity of Christ's teachings, so well matched by the ancient wisdom of the Tenth Commandment. It is one of the wonderful counterpoints of this age that the world's most famous woman was Mother Teresa, who chose the world's poorest city to work in. While the rest of us were paying court to the richest of the rich, she held up a dying baby or a sore-infested old man and asked us to look at the faces of the poorest of the poor.

Teresa walked with equal ease in the alleys of Calcutta and the salons of New York. She washed and comforted the bodies of the sick and dying and gave the poor the love they needed to believe in their own dignity and humanity as images of God. Her heart's treasure was with those who had nothing. She also begged worldwide for her dear ones and pointed out that the spiritual poverty of the wealthy needed ministry as well.

At the same time we need to nourish our minds and hearts with the social teachings of the Church. These will convert our hearts from being seduced by the rampant materialism of these days. The first step in acquiring a social conscience is the examination of our desires. Where is our treasure? Upon what do our hearts dwell? What are our basic attachments? When Christ's gospel has cleansed our hearts, then our minds will be cleared up about the genuine goals of life and society. This process prepares us to appreciate the Church's social teachings, which are nothing more than contemporary applications of Christ's gospel of detachment from material goods.

So we are urged to examine the state of our hearts. We should experience a "state of the heart" morality that is guided by gospel values and the Tenth Commandment. It used to be said that greed so affected the miners of the gold rush of 1849 that they mistook shiny dirt for gold. The illusion was called "fool's gold." Actually, even today's real gold is still "fool's gold" if it corrupts the souls of the owners and causes the poor of the world to lie forgotten and ignored at the glistening doors of gated communities and condominiums.

Jesus saw the same issues in his day when he told the story of Lazarus and the Rich Man. Poor Lazarus sat at the door of the wealthy man. He was too weak even to push away the dogs who licked his malnutrition sores. He ate the scraps that fell to the floor from the rich man's table. Eventually, Lazarus died and went to heaven. The rich man died and went to hell. He wasn't mean to the poor. He just never noticed them. He was too self-absorbed to even see the poor man on his doorstep. The love of money blinded him to people's needs.

MATTHEW 25:31-46

The drama of wealth and poverty is once again on the world's stage. We own the spiritual riches that could bring salvation to rich and poor alike. How long will it be before we do something about it?

Life Application

1) Review the various gospel teachings about poverty of spirit mentioned in this chapter. How do the teachings

of Jesus speak to you as you examine the state of your heart on these matters? In what way do you think you have been tempted to go along with the current cultural preoccupation with wealth? How does the quest for material goods affect family life, love between spouses and concern for the poor?

2) How would you describe the growing inequality caused in our culture by the new "zillionaires" and those in their wake? Besides the actual gap in dollars, what would be the best way to describe the psychological fallout due to this development? What would you say are immoral outcomes of this quest for money in the general fabric of our society—say, in media, family stability, respect for human dignity?

3) How often have you reflected on your heart's attachments, whether for good or ill? When you engage in such an exercise what effect does it have on your behavior? In what ways do you seem to have a real social conscience? Where could it improve? Who are role models that inspire you in this matter? Why have they influenced you?

• LEARN THE OPTION FOR THE POOR FROM THE STORY OF SAINT FRANCIS. (CCC, 2535-2540)

The attitude of wholesome detachment from material goods and the love of money may be acquired by the practice of generosity to others, especially to the poor. This option for the poor is recommended by the Church and exemplified in the life and teachings of Saint Francis of Assisi. In this section, we look at the Church's teaching and the witness of Saint Francis.

The Church has a centuries-old record of generosity to the stranger, the widow and the orphan. Followers of Jesus are responsible for hospitals, shelters, child-care facilities, hospices and schools. The Second Vatican Council reconfirmed this mission of generosity:

> [T]he Church encompasses with love all those who are afflicted with human weakness. Indeed, she recognizes in the poor and suffering the likeness of her poor and suffering Founder. She does all she can to relieve their need and in them she strives to serve Christ. (*Constitution on the Church*, 8)

Generosity has attained a new expressiveness in our time as the pope and bishops call the Catholic people to a "preferential option for the poor." The concept developed in Latin America among those working in the thousands of new small faith communities (*communidades de base*). Of course, it is founded in Scripture, especially in the Prophets and the teachings of Jesus. It draws attention to the millions upon millions of poor people packed in barrios around the major cities of Latin America. Anyone driving from the airports of Sao Paulo, Lima or Mexico City on the way into the center of the cities will pass through miles of such barrios. To speak of a preferential option for these people is to say that their need should be a top priority for the Church.

In a letter to the Brazilian bishops, Pope John Paul II expressed his solidarity with them as they seek to minister to so vast a population of poor people:

> The Church witnesses the fact that human dignity must not be destroyed, whatever the situation of poverty, scorn, rejection or powerlessness to which a human being has been reduced.
>
> She shows her solidarity with those who do not count in a society by which they are rejected spiritually and sometimes even physically. She is particularly drawn with maternal affection towards those children who, through human wickedness, will never be brought forth from the womb to the light of day, as also for the elderly, alone and abandoned. The special option for the poor...manifests the universality of the Church's being and mission. (*Instruction on Christian Freedom and Liberation*, 68)

The pope's first concern in these words is about the human dignity of all the world's poor: the economically impoverished, the politically oppressed, those who count for nothing in a society. He asks all Catholics to stand in solidarity with those so oppressed. He includes the aborted, the elderly, the lonely and abandoned.

The special option for the poor does not exclude a ministry to every Catholic and a mission effort to all the world. But it should motivate us to speak up for the deprived and participate in methods designed to reform the societal evils that oppress the poor. Any reformation of structure must also include converting the hearts of the people who administer the institutions.

Even if we reform the structures, there is no guarantee of justice unless the people managing them make personal choices that put the structures at the service of the poor. Hence a Christian conversion of heart is essential to making the structures of society truly serve the needs of the poor.

Francis' Story

Such conversion, the ability to be a giver, is a gift from God. It is a grace resulting from a divine call, human openness to the possibility and the consequent willingness to accept it in faith. In Saint Francis of Assisi, this dynamic appears vividly, though it should be remembered that the same process occurs in less dramatic form in all good people who enjoy the vocation of giver.

There are many parallels between the thirteenth-century culture that bred Saint Francis and our own times. His age witnessed a revival of commerce, which caused a shift in population, along with a new concentration of wealth. Large masses of people left rural areas and flooded the cities. Huge numbers of homeless people encircled the city walls. These pitiful, displaced poor people huddled near the bastions of the rich. The Church needed a new method for reaching the masses of poor people clustered around the walls of old medieval cities and new towns. It found the answer in the life and ministry of Francis of Assisi.

The son of a prosperous cloth merchant, Francis was a city person, gifted with a friendly personality, a voracious love of life and a poetic temperament. He had the capacity for loving whatever he was doing—indulging in the latest fashions, long nights of partying or simply being with people. He identified with the prevailing romantic ideals of the noble warrior: chivalrous, courteous and generous to the defeated.

It was in this spirit that he became a soldier in the perennial battles between Assisi and neighboring Perugia. His brief career in the military, which included defeat and imprisonment, disillusioned him. The viciousness of mortal combat, the naked hatred of the adversaries and the numbing humiliations of his jail cell brought him to a moment of truth and the experience of radical self-evaluation.

Like the rich young man of the Gospel, he felt he was being called by Jesus to a new way of living. Unlike that Gospel man, Francis said yes to Jesus. When he saw the hordes of the poor milling like sheep without a shepherd, he resolved to take Christ's call seriously and literally rid himself of all worldly possessions. He sensed that absolute solidarity and identification with the poor was the only way to help them.

Brave enough to engage in hand-to-hand combat, he found within himself the moral courage to let go of his wealth, security and family power base. Remaining the romantic, Francis switched from wanting to be a military hero doing brave deeds for the woman of his dreams to being a spiritual warrior dedicated to "Lady Poverty."

His break with his family contained all the perennial elements that characterize misunderstanding between a son and his parents: anger, harsh words, love lamely expressed, fixed and immovable counterpositions. The bishop tried to heal the rift between son and father, summoning them both to a meeting at his residence. There Francis disrobed, symbolizing his rejection of his inheritance and his newfound solidarity with the naked and poor of the world, as well as with the Christ who had nowhere to lay his head. He then set forth on his mission to the poor with a view to helping them find human dignity and a better way of life.

Barefoot and penniless, he preached trust in God and called people to enjoy the wonders and beauties of nature, God's masterpieces, free to everyone and designed to charm and expand the soul. He dedicated himself in part to the service of the most despised, of people suffering from leprosy. He invited rich and poor alike to experience the unique pleasures of letting go of what impeded their spiritual growth and permitting the grace of God and the beauty of the universe to flow into their souls. Everyone could be renewed by the creative energies of Brother Sun and Sister Moon.

Soon he attracted crowds to hear his messages, and a small circle of disciples adopted his evangelical lifestyle. This new group aroused the suspicion of Church authorities, who wondered if this was another version of the disruptive "Poor Men of Lyons," who had been discredited 40 years earlier.

That group had started innocently enough, living in communes, earning their living by weaving and other urban trades. They pursued a simple lifestyle, opposed the amassing of wealth, avoided taverns and dancing and practiced celibacy. They looked a lot like the later Puritans. They liked to take the pulpits in the churches and give sermons on the Bible, from which they cited only texts that dealt with poverty and hard work.

Trouble arose when they proceeded to attack the luxurious lifestyles of the bishops and the clergy, alienating the people from them. They did not stop there, but went further, declaring they were the only real Christians, that the pope and bishops were sources of error, that the sacraments were useless and simply evil means for financing the Church. The pope banned them. The secular powers disbanded them as a threat to the social order. They disappeared as a significant social or spiritual presence.

Francis knew that he must show the pope that he and his brothers were not going in that direction. He went to Rome, met with Innocent III, convinced him of the merit of his mission and received the pope's oral approval.

The friars then experienced an enormous growth. They preached everywhere. Populist in approach, they presented a Christianity for the urban poor that was a mixture of penance and self-discipline—just the right mix of values to help the poor get to heaven, as well as to get on the first step to upward mobility and a humane way of life.

Francis proved to be a social reformer consistent with the temper of his culture. He appealed to people's self-worth and taught them the planning attitudes that would lift them out of the poverty cycle while also nourishing their souls with the virtues of trust and faith. Part of his appeal was his exuberant use of the romantic imagery of chivalry. He knew his listeners' idiom and used it effectively. He avoided the thunderous style of a Jeremiah or Amos; he was evocative rather than provocative. He could charm the rich so that they conceded their need to have at least some solidarity with the poor. He enraptured the poor with both heavenly and earthly dreams that insisted on human dignity without abandoning simplicity—in fact convincing them that simplicity was essential to that dignity. His loving treatment of lepers seems like it leaps from the pages of the Gospels.

Francis bluntly used the cultural conceits of his times, but he was far from being the soft, mellow figure of the Giotto paintings. He was vulnerable to the sufferings of the vast army of the poor. He absorbed their pain as well as the pain of the passion of Jesus, whose wounds he received in the stigmata.

When he came to die, he asked to be laid on the earth that he might have the closest possible touch with the creation through which he had seen the Creator so vividly.

There is no record as to which commandment was Francis' favorite. But there is no doubt that, better than any other Christian since Christ himself, Francis exemplified the spirit of poverty that is so well recommended by the Tenth Commandment. By the end of his life there was clearly not a covetous bone in his body. Francis was consummately the man of the last commandment.

His celebrated witness to poverty of spirit, which includes generosity, a preferential option for the poor and a stewardship that understands that only in giving do we receive, rescues this ideal from being a mere abstraction. Doubtless, we expect Jesus to be so generous. But is it possible for any other human being? Francis proved that it is. So have many other Christians before and since, sometimes in visible, dramatic ways, more often in simple, modest and touching ways that will never be chronicled.

For Dialogue

1) How could the adoption of generous hearts help us overcome the love of money and attachment to worldly goods?

2) Why does the Church urge us to have a "preferential option for the poor"?

3) Why could we say that self-made successful people may be more likely to be caring for the poor? How true is this?

4) At the same time, it has often been noticed that the poor are frequently more generous hearted than the rich. If this be true, why is it so?

5) What have you learned from the life of Saint Francis that would enable you to follow gospel teaching about poverty of spirit and the intention of the Tenth Commandment?

- **BE GENEROUS AND REMOVE DISORDERED DESIRES**. (*CCC*, 2534, 2548-2557)

Generosity is a condition for happiness. The Old Testament prophets tried to awaken it in their people. The first chapter of Isaiah pictures the prophet addressing a temple audience with a view to touching their consciences about the poor. Isaiah is in no mood to be tactful. He begins by calling the people the moral equivalent of Sodom and Gomorrah.

He lectures them at length on the superficiality of their worship. He tells them that God cares little for the multitude of sacrifices, that he is fed up with the fat of bulls and the blood of lambs. God finds the incense loathsome and the festivals at the new moon unbearable.

> When you spread out your hands,/ I close my eyes to you..../Your hands are full of blood! (Isaiah 1:15)

These are sturdy words for that respectable, temple-going audience. Isaiah's tone changes at this point. Heartfelt appeal to their better natures replaces the fire and brimstone. Though their hands are full of blood, they can wash themselves clean. How? By permitting the humanitarian impulse to surface. They should redress the wrongs they have committed, hear the orphan's plea and the cry of the widow. Isaiah approaches the congregation with gentle intimacy:

> Come now, let us set things right,/says the LORD:/ Though your sins be like scarlet,/they may become white as snow;/Though they be crimson red,/they may become white as wool. (Isaiah 1:18)

Isaiah explains to them that God wants a change of attitude toward what can well be called the humanitarian impulse. This kind of prophetic evangelizing found its way into scriptural ideals of humanitarian generosity. The best-known practical implementation in biblical times was the sabbatical year. Just as every seventh day was a sabbath, so every seventh year was declared a sabbath year.

A description of the sabbatical year may be found in Deuteronomy 15:1-18. One of Israel's biggest social problems was poverty caused by losing property because of inability to repay the loans used to purchase the land. Moreover, those who defaulted on their debts were often forced to be slaves until the debt was repaid by years of labor.

That destroyed the social equality that had existed when the people were all members of tribes in a nomadic society. The sabbatical year was meant to be a time when debts were canceled and slaves freed. This social amnesty, based on the imitation of God's forgiving generosity, was designed to give people a new lease on life and restore their social equality. The custom grew out of a prophetic appeal for generosity and sowed a humanitarian impulse that has been an enduring feature of Judaism and Christianity alike. It is reflected today in the pope's plea for the forgiveness of the debts of poor nations.

In his *The Gospel of Matthew,* Scripture commentator William Barclay points out that the Jewish rabbis in biblical times laid down five guidelines for giving:

1) One should accept a gift and not refuse it.

2) The giver (or giving community) should offer a family more than what is needed to keep body and soul together. The family should receive enough to get it back on its feet in society.

3) Where possible, the giving should be secret. The noblest form of giving is when the giver does not know who the receiver is and the receiver is unaware of who did the giving.

4) The giver should be sensitive about the feelings and pride of the recipient. The manner of giving is as important as the gift.

5) Giving is a privilege as well as an obligation, for in giving to a needy person one gives to God. The person who befriends the poor lends to the Lord and will

receive a similar kindness from God.

These laws of giving reflect the positive spirit of the commandment that draws people away from a greedy attitude so that they may adopt a generous one.

The spirit and the letter of the Tenth Commandment liberate us from avarice. It deals with the unrestrained love of money that is the root of all the evils forbidden in the other nine covenant rules. An avaricious attitude leads people to murder, lie, steal and abandon the elderly. Some greedy people collect their piles of gold and expect sex as a reward. The avaricious person strays from God and religion and loses respect for the divine and the human person alike. "[P]eople in their desire for [money] have strayed from the faith…" (1 Timothy 6:10b).

The Tenth Commandment challenges us to acquire the value of generosity in our attitudinal life. By diverting us from greed, avarice and all forms of undue possessiveness, it opens the broad avenues of the altruistic heart. The attitude of generosity is biblically based and dear to the heart of Christ. People in need of every kind appeal to our capacity to be givers. Once we try it, we find out there is more pleasure in giving than receiving. We make the further gratifying discovery that there is an unexpected joy of receiving in the very act of giving. Then we know that generosity is better than greed any day.

The last commandment balances the first one. If the first speaks of the need for faith in God, the final commandment urges the covenant person to acquire the spirit of Christian generosity. Generosity negates the greed that tempts us to abandon covenant love with God, self and others, as well as all the commandments that express such love.

Reflection

1) Medieval monks had a saying: "Diligence begets abundance. Abundance begets laxity. Laxity begets

189

decadence." What applicability does their saying have today? How is our abundant affluence making us morally lax?

2) Read again the five laws of giving on pages 188-189. How do they apply to your life today?

3) Asked what he planned to do with the prestigious education he was receiving at one of America's elite universities, one student replied: "I want power. I want to be in charge of a large company and see what I can do with it. I assure you I will not do anything illegal to get what I want—a million-dollar home, a BMW and all that power. I'd do whatever I had to do without breaking the law, but I'd probably be pretty slimy. I know it's the 'in' thing to care about human life, but—don't push me any further on that."

Is lust for power substantially different from financial greed? What would you say to this student? If you were this student's religion teacher, what challenge would you present to him?

Meditation

The passion for power and money corrupts the human heart. There is a Roman proverb that says money is like sea water. The more a man drinks of it, the thirstier he gets. Luke's Gospel tells the story of a rich fool who tore down all his barns and built bigger ones to hold the increase of his bountiful harvests. Afterward he smugly contented himself and said to himself, "Now as for you, you have so many good things stored up for many years, rest, eat, drink, be merry!" (Luke 12:19).

God had a different plan for him. "You fool, this night your life will be demanded of you; and the things you have prepared, to whom will they belong?" (Luke 12:20).

It is all a matter of attitudes and priorities. Jesus cautions us to avoid a possessive attitude. The first priority should be the kingdom of God, which means aiming for a life of love, justice and mercy. Saints like Katherine Drexel, Thomas More and Francis of Assisi were able to have a laid-back attitude toward worldly possessions. This enabled them to fashion a vision and witness that has inspired millions of people. The more this attitude prevails, the better world we will have.

When we leave this earth, the only things we will take with us are those we have given away.

Prayer

Generous God, you have poured your abundance into creation for our benefit. You have given each of us the potential for happiness so long as we use your gifts for the purpose you had in mind. Help us to put aside all envy and greed and replace these attitudes with those of generosity and selfless giving. Save us from the materialism of our culture and nourish us with the food of higher virtues. Teach us to practice the maxim, "It is in giving that we receive." AMEN.

Wisdom is knowing what to do. Skill is knowing how to do it. Virtue is doing it. (Thomas Jefferson)